PROPHETS, GUARDIANS, AND SAINTS

Shapers of Modern Catholic History

Owen F. Cummings

Paulist Press
New York/Mahwah, NJ

With gratitude to Father Michael Kerrigan, CSP, my editor, and to Jeska Kobelski, my copyeditor, for all their work.

"God's Grandeur" and "As Kingfishers Catch Fire" from *The Poems of Gerard Manley Hopkins,* by Gerard Manley Hopkins, edited by Gardner, W. H. & MacKenzie, N. H. (1970). By permission of Oxford University Press on behalf of the British Province of the Society of Jesus.

Photo of George Tyrrell, courtesy of San Francisco Gleeson Library Archives.

Cover design by Joy Taylor
Book design by Lynn Else

Library of Congress Cataloging-in-Publication Data

Cummings, Owen F.
Prophets, guardians, and saints : shapers of modern Catholic history / Owen F. Cummings.
    p.   cm.
Includes bibliographical references.
ISBN 978-0-8091-4446-4 (alk. paper)
1. Catholic—Biography. I. Title.
BX4651.3.C86 2007
282.09'034—dc22

2006037761

Published by Paulist Press
997 Macarthur Boulevard
Mahwah, New Jersey 07430

www.paulistpress.com

Printed and bound in the
United States of America

CONTENTS

For
Seymour B. House
Cor ad cor loquitur

INTRODUCTION

This introductory work owes a great deal in approach, method, and inspiration to a scholar who is insufficiently known in the United States. Her name is Meriol Trevor (1919–2000). Trevor is probably best known as a writer of children's books, but she authored two books that speak particularly to the concerns of nineteenth-century church history and theology: *Newman's Journey,* bringing together her earlier two-volume biography of Newman;[1] and *Prophets and Guardians: Renewal and Tradition in the Church.*[2] *Newman's Journey* is an excellent biography, laced with numerous quotations from Newman's books, letters, and sermons. Trevor had access to the then unpublished data housed in Newman's Oratory on the Hagley Road, Birmingham. *Prophets and Guardians* is a splendid guide through the intricacies of the nineteenth-century church.

Thus, Meriol Trevor's shade stands over this volume. Who was she? Born in London in 1919, Trevor read classics and philosophy at St. Hugh's College, Oxford, at the same time as her friend, Dame Iris Murdoch, the philosopher and novelist. As a result of reading the Anglican apologist C. S. Lewis, Trevor moved to Christianity and became a Roman Catholic in 1950. Like Murdoch, she gave over much of her life to writing, but in fact, though she did not advertise it, she lived and died in poverty in her apartment in Bath, England.[3]

Trevor was an advocate of tradition, and she is very clear what she means by that: "I think it a shallow view to equate tradition with conservatism (political and intellectual), with monarchic views of Church organization and the rejection of all ideas and ideals which arise from other sources than those approved by the Vatican. The fraternal tradition is at least as old as the paternal. It has never ceased in the Church. It cannot cease, for it is of its essence."[4] Here is no adolescent rejection of authority or of the magisterium—no Catholic can dismiss the importance and the centrality of the Petrine ministry and the magisterium, and certainly Meriol Trevor never did—but simply the recognition that tradition is wider and richer than magisterial directives and pronouncements. Tradition is composed of both *prophets* and *guardians.* To use contemporary language, prophets are progressives, guardians are conservatives. However, it is not simply a matter of personal endorsement, or of personal preference, as Trevor points out:

> Prophets can go astray and become false prophets. Guardians, in their zeal to preserve unity of mind and heart in the community, can sometimes fail to imitate the patience of God who allows men to work out their lives in freedom....Because Christianity is a communion of persons, it must also be a communion of ideas....It is not a question of discarding doctrine, but of enlarging the concepts, seeing them in the setting of our later world. But because the Church is a very large society, with many peoples living at different stages of psychological development within it, it seems likely to be a very slow process."[5]

Here is a rich view of tradition as the church perpetually renewing itself, handing itself over to the next generation, directed and inspired by both its prophets and its guardians. It informs the perspective of this modest book.

In Meriol Trevor's words, the family struggle between prophets and guardians is constant. The study of history invites us to recognize this so that we might gain insight and perspective. The study of church history invites us to gain insight and perspective not only into the past but also into the present of the church—indeed, into the present of ourselves. There is a wonderful subchapter entitled "Truth and Tradition," in *Prophets and Guardians*. There we find the sentence: "People are not embodied ideas, right or wrong all through from start to finish. The Church is people."[6] The church was people in the past, and the church is people today. Insight and perspective concerning the church are best yielded through a study of the people of the church, and so this book is devoted largely to a study of nineteenth-century people and their ideas. No such study may pretend to completeness.

The late Alec R. Vidler, the Anglican theologian and historian of modernism, once wrote: "I am much less confident than I used to be of my capacity to understand other people." He goes on to cite some words of Max Beerbohm: "Posterity, I hope, will be puzzled what to think about anybody. How baffling and contradictory are our most intimate and contemporary friends! And how many of us can gauge even himself!"[7] Thus, as we attempt to gain insight into the Catholic Church of the nineteenth century, we end not with a period but with a comma, as it were. There is always more to be said. It is for that reason that at the end of each chapter a brief bibliography is given. It is the author's hope that some small contribution will be made to self-understanding in the church and as church in the twenty-first century.

Notes

1. Meriol Trevor, *Newman, Pillar of the Cloud* (Garden City, NY: Doubleday, 1962), and Newman, *Light in Winter* (Garden City, NY: Doubleday, 1962).

2. Meriol Trevor, *Prophets and Guardians: Renewal and Tradition in the Church* (London/Sydney/Toronto: Hollis and Carter, 1969).

3. Eldred Willey, "Obituary of Meriol Trevor," *The Tablet* (January 22, 2000): 98.

4. Trevor, *Prophets and Guardians,* 9.

5. Ibid., 10–12.

6. Ibid., 89.

7. Alec R. Vidler, *A Variety of Catholic Modernists* (Cambridge: Cambridge University Press, 1970), 21.

1
JOHANN ADAM MÖHLER (1796–1838)

Johann Adam Möhler was the light of the Tübingen school, neither dry-as-dust nor an inflated metaphysical balloon, but a scholar and thinker whose unusual personal charm is as evident in his works as in his letters. —Alexander Dru[1]

Catholicism in the mid-twentieth century prior to Vatican Council II (1962–1965) was largely narrow, defensive, and reactionary—the church *contra mundum,* against the world, and the world included Protestants, secularists, and atheists. Ecclesiology was clear in that context. One's ecclesial and even cultural identity was shaped and molded by this defensive Catholicism through regular attendance and participation in the sacraments of the church. "Confession," the term for the sacrament of penance and reconciliation, was, for all practical purposes in the experience of ordinary Catholics, a form of control of moral impulses in a challenging environment, and especially in the area of sexuality. From a scholarly point of view, one might wish to nuance and fine-tune this picture, but it is no caricature. It was a fortress-like church, and personal experience was too often taken up with the mechanics of the externals. It was a ghetto Catholicism. Lay alongside this the theology and the ecclesiology, now over one hundred years old, of Johann Adam Möhler, and one immediately sees the liberating perspective for which Möhler stands.

The liberation of theology and, implicitly, of ecclesiology represented by the Tübingen School, with Möhler as its best exemplar, is sketched nicely by Cardinal Walter Kasper:

1

A return to the ghetto of the old theology of the school is out of the question. In the long term, the developments of recent years have brought too many positive and promising new approaches....If Catholic theology is to survive at all, it has to free itself completely from the fetters of the neo-scholastic system. Theology—especially theology in the tradition of the Tübingen Catholic school—is possible only in the open river of time.[2]

Möhler was certainly unfettered by neo-scholasticism and was open to the developments of his day. He offered, and continues to offer, a way of doing theology and ecclesiology that is excitingly Catholic.

Early Years

Johann Adam Möhler, the son of a baker and innkeeper, was born on May 6, 1796, in the village of Igersheim, some thirty miles south of Würzburg, Germany. Starting in 1813, Möhler was educated at the high school in Ellwangen, but before attending class every day he helped his father bake for several hours. The Möhler scholar Herve Savon comments that discipline at the Lyceum of Ellwangen was not at its best: "The inns were full of students who ensconced themselves there from three in the afternoon until closing time."[3] Möhler had no room for the inn! He was a fine student, but his years at Ellwangen were not free of personal stress. He seems to have passed through a personal crisis, at first deciding not to move toward the priesthood and to take up law instead. This may have had to do with his father's reluctant approval of the priesthood as his vocation, as well as difficult financial circumstances. He passed through this crisis and moved to the Catholic Faculty of Theology in the University of Tübingen in 1817. Savon also tells us something of the situation in Tübingen: "There was much discussion there of abolishing ecclesiastical celibacy, a step the seminarians enthusiastically advocated. For most of them, who came from very poor families, the priesthood was primarily a way of making a living."[4] After moving to the seminary of Rotenburg in 1818, Möhler was ordained a priest on September 18, 1819. He spent a year working in pastoral ministry before returning to the University of Tübingen in 1820.

The Catholic Faculty of Theology at Tübingen was open to dialogue with the various movements of the day, both secular and Protestant. They also tended to view the church organically rather than primarily in structural and hierarchical terms. Their approach to theology was more historical than philosophical, and when they did appropriate philosophy, it tended to be Idealism, and especially that of Schelling. Perhaps the best example is Johann Sebastian Drey (1777–1853), often referred to as the "father" of the Catholic Tübingen School. Drey had been appointed to Ellwangen to teach dogma and apologetics in 1812 and would have known Möhler there before moving with him to Tübingen in 1813. Using Schelling's philosophy, Drey saw creation as first revelation. This provided him with an organic view of history from the beginning, centered on the kingdom of God, fully expressed in the history of the church. "It was Drey, perhaps more than any other Tübingen theologian of the day, who stimulated the young Möhler's work at the time he was writing the *Unity*."[5]

The German Tour

Before taking up a formal teaching position at Tübingen, Möhler went on a tour of the German schools, as was the scholarly custom of the day. The journey, paid for mostly by his uncle Philipp Joseph von Messner (1763–1835), took him to Göttingen, Breslau, Leipzig, Halle, and other centers. Savon judges that "[t]his journey…through Germany may well have been the decisive event in his formation."[6] Perhaps his greatest attraction was in the newly established University of Berlin, where he spent three weeks. There the young Möhler came across the two great teachers who, in their different ways were to exercise considerable influence on him—Friedrich D. E. Schleiermacher (1768–1834) and Joachim Neander (1789–1850). Neander's lectures in patristic theology and Schleiermacher's approach to systematic theology were both marked by organic images of the body to describe the Christian church and showed the young Möhler what a living theology could be, in contrast to desiccated rationalism and polemics. Neander especially impressed him with both his knowledge of and his love for the tradition and history of the church. Möhler wrote of him:

> His character is worthy of love and unpretentious in the highest degree. In Berlin he knows no streets except those that lead to the university, and no person except his colleagues. But Origen, Tertullian, Augustine, Chrysostom, St. Bernard, the letters of Boniface, and many others, he knows by heart.[7]

When his German tour was over, Möhler became professor of church history at Tübingen in 1828.

The Last Years

He moved to the University of Munich as professor in 1835. The great Catholic historian Ignaz von Döllinger (1799–1890) taught at the university and later was to become both a supporter and the editor of Möhler's collected works. Very soon, however, he found himself alone and in poor health. The following year he was attacked by cholera. The year 1837 saw him renouncing teaching altogether on the grounds of his poor health. He was appointed by King Louis I of Bavaria a canon of Würzburg Cathedral, but he died on April 12, 1838.

Herve Savon writes: "In his last hours, he expressed one final regret: at being unable to write the book in which he would at last have expressed what he now knew and what he had seen."[8]

Möhler on Canon Law and Liturgy

One of Möhler's initial obligations in the theology faculty at Tübingen was teaching canon law. It is in these lectures, and in reviews in the periodical *Theologische Quartalschrift,* established by the professors of Tübingen in 1819, that we first come across his ecclesiology. In 1823 he wrote a review of Ferdinand Walter's *Manual of Canon Law.* Walter was a professor of canon law at the University of Bonn, and Möhler was using this textbook in class. There Möhler attacked what he called "the papal system," a papally centered view of the church, favored by Walter over against an episcopally centered view of the church, Möhler's own preference at this time. He was opposed to the notion of papal infallibility. This was fifty-seven years before the definition of infallibility of the First Vatican Council (1870), and it was a matter of theological debate. In Möhler's view the pope can err in matters of faith as judged by the universal church, and so by an ecumenical council. A doctrine is approved by an ecumenical council, representing the faith of the universal—that is, Catholic—church. If a doctrine is not believed by the universal church, it is not Catholic, and the pope's saying so cannot make it so. The episcopal system, expressed in council, is superior to the papal system.

In the same review article, Möhler advocated the liturgy in German over Latin. The canonist Walter saw Latin as an expression of unity and as a common language in the church. Not so for Möhler: "Fine unity, a unity in incomprehension!"[9] In a subsequent article on missions in the same review, Möhler consistently argued for a vernacular liturgy over a Latin one.

Consciousness of God

In 1825, again in the periodical *Theologische Quartalschrift,* Möhler reviewed a work by theologian Adam Gengler, entitled *On the Relationship of Theology to Philosophy.* Gengler espoused the distinction between knowledge and faith, a distinction that did not entirely please Möhler. In Möhler's response to Gengler we find a major principle of his theology:

> The idea of God is a fact of consciousness, and what could be more evident to us than such a fact?...If the idea of God is based in an impulse of our spiritual nature, of our deepest being, if I grasp myself in this impulse and give it the form of a representation, how can this not reflect an existent? How can it not be knowledge?[10]

In Möhler's understanding, an understanding that was to pervade his entire *oeuvre,* faith is not assenting to something told one by another. Faith, rather, is a fact of consciousness. It springs forth from within.

Unity in the Church

Michael Himes, an American expert on Möhler, writes: "Möhler deserves to be regarded as the creator of ecclesiology as a field within systematic...theology."[11] Möhler's first major book, *Unity in the Church,* is best thought of as a conversation with the great Friedrich Schleiermacher. Möhler sent a copy of the book with a cover letter to his good friend Joseph Lipp, and in this letter we get a sense of how the book came to be written:

> A careful study of the Fathers has stirred up much in me. While undertaking it I discovered for the first time a living, fresh, full Christianity, and Christ

desires that I do not leave fruitless that which he gave life to and awakened for his full defense.[12]

Out of his study of the patristic period—and every page of *Unity in the Church* reflects it—emerge a strongly relational anthropology, ecclesiology, and pneumatology. Unity in the Church is divided into two parts. The first part is taken up with the inner life or Spirit of the church. What Möhler means by "Spirit" is all-important, as the German counterpart, *Geist,* in a post-Hegel world could mean a range of things. Hegel's most important work was his *Phenomenology of Spirit,* and *Geist* is the German for "spirit." Möhler was aware of Hegel's *Geist.* "Spirit" for him is both a way of speaking of the divine transcendence-immanence, and also of the Holy Spirit, making and forming the union of all Christian believers. This means that the Spirit's communion with all believers brings about a real participation in the life of the divine communion:

> The foundation of the Church on faith in the Trinity was not possible without the communication of the Holy Spirit and could not have continued without the Spirit's preservation of it; this is the Spirit's work and the only thing worthy of its power and majesty. Together all believers form an organic whole. By the different communication of one and the same Spirit according to the different needs and characteristics of each person, all are directed to each other and are, together, members completing one another.[13]

Thus, there is what we might call vertical communion with the Trinity through the Spirit, and simultaneously horizontal communion with all humankind, sacramentalized in the communion of the church. The second part of the book is engaged with the external and visible form of the church. It examines the external, corporate expressions of unity through personal communion between people and the bishop, between bishops in episcopal collegiality, and between the bishops and the pope.

The following passage gives one a feel for Möhler's organic and corporate approach:

> A human being is set in a great whole to act and to view himself or herself as a *member* in it. One must acknowledge this relationship and dare neither oppose oneself to the whole nor set oneself above it....Thus, just as each individual in the whole is grounded in God, God can be known by the individual only in the whole....Thus, although the individual is not the whole, the whole is yet in the individual and the individual knows what the whole is....How is the single individual to know (God)? Only because the individual, although not the whole, can yet *embrace it with great mind, with love.* Thus, although the individual *is* not the whole, the whole is yet in the individual, and the individual knows what the whole is. We, as individual essences, expand ourselves to the whole in love. Love grasps God.[14]

Viewed from this perspective, the doctrines of the faith are not first and foremost objective propositions to be held onto extrinsically, but rather they are the articulation of intrinsic Christian experience.

> Christianity does not consist in expressions, formulae or figures of speech; it is an inner life, a holy power, and all doctrinal concepts and dogmas have value only insofar as they express the inner life that is present with them.[15]

Doctrine, then, expresses the concrete experience of the believing subject-in-community. Viewed from this perspective, heresy is atomism, individualism, egoism, a disconnection from the whole.

> For [the heretics] the individual precedes the community, and unity is set aside. For heretics, the individual must seek truth according to the pattern that the individual alone establishes and must therefore be free from all faith commitments in that seeking.[16]

The opposite of heresy is tradition, the common consciousness of Christianity.

There are two basic styles or forms of theology, the mystical-contemplative and the speculative-analytic. Möhler compares them to the experience of music:

> If music is to be heard, it can only be received by individuals in its total impression, in the blending of the different tones of instruments and voices. Individuals can, after they have heard the music, break it down into its individual parts and note closely what association of individual elements beget a particular sound, according to what laws it operated, and what can yet be heard from these. The mystic rejoices in the glorious harmonic play that Christianity brings forth in its inner life in its totality. The mystic lives in intuition in unmediated, spiritual tasting, and considers it a disturbance of this, a weakening and a removal of it, if one proposes to analyze it. The speculative theologian takes up analysis. *But the speculative theologian must have heard the harmony and received it* for himself or herself. Or such a theologian is speaking of something foreign and does not know of what he or she is speaking.[17]

One contemporary commentator says: "Schleiermacher's work *The Christian Faith* might conceivably have been given the

9

same title as Möhler's book, *Unity in the Church.* Ecclesiology provides the starting point and the framework for the whole of Schleiermacher's theology, with the Church's unity providing one of its most pervasive themes."[18] There was a pervasive tendency in Schleiermacher to disparage the institutional and dogmatic elements of Christianity and to give primary emphasis to religious experience. In part, this was to make Christianity appeal to its many cultured despisers, but, though Möhler feels the pull of this position, he does not succumb to its allurements in quite the same way. He recognizes the Holy Spirit building up the church as communion. "The Church exists through a life directly and continually moved by the divine Spirit, and is maintained and continued by the loving, mutual exchange of believers."[19] The entire external apparatus of the church is an expression of the interior belief and working of the Holy Spirit in the hearts and minds of believers, corporately and individually. The church is defined from the inside, as it were, from this work of the Holy Spirit in the hearts of believers. This contrasts sharply with a centuries-old emphasis on the externality of the church that grew up in response to the perceived invisibility of the church among the Reformers. It comes into clear relief when Möhler speaks of the meaning of ordination.

> According to its external appearance the ordination is nothing other than the acknowledgement of the whole Church that her Spirit is in a specific believer and that this Spirit makes that believer worthy to represent the love of a specific number of believers and to join them with the whole Church. In the ordination, the Holy Spirit is not so much first communicated as it is acknowledged that specific gifts have been *earlier* communicated to the one who is to be ordained.[20]

Yet again we see the inner-outer dynamic at work.

On Priesthood and Celibacy

In 1826 an article by Möhler appeared in the journal *Theologische Quartalschrift* entitled "Some Thoughts on the Diminishing Number of Priests and Certain Related Questions." As a result of the secularizing tendencies of the French Revolution, fewer men were presenting themselves for ordination. Understandably enough this caused much distress, but not for Möhler. His patristic studies led him to see that historically there were just as many priests as service to actual Christian communities demanded. The phenomenon of excessive numbers of priests grew out of an unhealthy emphasis on the multiplication of Masses as history moved through the medieval period. Möhler maintained that the reduction in numbers was a cause not for regret but for joy. Here is the nucleus of his argument:

> From the very nature of things, there can only be few priests. For only those are really priests of God who have received the breath of the divine Spirit, the holy kiss, the consecration of the mind, the unction of the heart...those who are silent in the sanctuary if God himself does not loose their tongue....How many of them can there be? Think of celibacy. How few there are who are able and eager to understand it. Even if in this respect there are to outward appearances many priests, interiorly there are very few.[21]

His sentiments here have a very contemporary ring to them.

Symbolism

Möhler's book *Symbolism* was very influential both in the nineteenth century and in the first part of the twentieth. It was reprinted sixteen times before 1914 and was translated from

German into Latin, Italian, French, Dutch, Swedish and Polish, as well as English. The reasons for its influence and success may be found in the fact that it offered "a dignified defense of the Catholic Church's theological anthropology, sacramental theology, and ecclesiology not only in comparison with various branches of Protestantism, but also in contrast to modern rationalists and naturalists."[22]

In this book he moved away from an excessive emphasis on the Holy Spirit found in his *Unity in the Church* toward a more christological or christocentric emphasis. We may observe this shift of perspective in a famous text from Möhler's *Symbolism:*

> Thus, the visible Church, from the point of view here taken, is the Son of God himself, everlastingly manifesting himself among men in a human form, perpetually renovated, and eternally young—the permanent incarnation of the same, as in Holy Writ, even the faithful are called "the body of Christ." Hence, it is evident that the Church, though composed of men, is yet not purely human.[23]

What we have here and in other parts of the later editions of *Symbolism* is not so much a repudiation of his earlier pneumatology as a trinitarian expansion to give due place to the person of Christ. In his fine book *Communion Ecclesiology,* Dennis Doyle contrasts *Unity* as offering a "low, ascending ecclesiology," while *Symbolism* is marked by a "high, descending ecclesiology."[24] Both books seem to me to advocate a high ecclesiology. The Spirit is no human project, and in that sense *Unity* is not "low." Christ equally is God in the flesh and is not a human construct. Both ecclesiologies are "high," but perhaps in *Unity* we see a more organic approach based on the Spirit, while in *Symbolism* the ongoing incarnation of Christ in the church seems more immediately divine.

Some Critical Thoughts

While Möhler's Spirit-centered ecclesiology, or his Christ/ Body-centered ecclesiology is liberating when contrasted with juridical ecclesiologies, or defensive ecclesiologies, it is not without problems. These problems are not as such found in Möhler, but in possible extremist versions that develop out of his ecclesiology.

Perhaps the immediate problem has to do with the possible collapse of the Spirit into the church. The power of his language could quite easily be taken in this direction, though it is not Möhler's own path. One could end up with an immanentism, not far removed from pantheism. Again, if the Holy Spirit is the animator of the church in the exciting ways in which Möhler describes, one might end up with an "ecclesiological monophysitism." Like its christological counterpart in the history of doctrine, this monophysitism of the church does not adequately take into account the human aspect. The church may become too divinized, as it were.

Similarly, this ecclesiological monophysitism may, especially through Möhler's treatment of heresy, silence critical voices that need to be heard in the church. These are the prophetic voices of every generation that summon the church to look more closely at its performance and witness. Dorothy Day would fall into this category, as would many of the liberation theologians of Latin America and Asia. If the church is regarded as too perfect, it need not listen to such voices, and her witness would be diminished. I do not believe this would happen in Möhler's own theology and ecclesiology, because for him the Spirit is *everywhere* in the church. Checks and balances are present in its organic development. But in the hands of the less able, checks and balances do not seem especially necessary.

Conclusion

Möhler's influence did not die with him. With the neo-scholastic revival toward the end of the nineteenth century and the beginning of the twentieth, the works of Möhler were largely ignored until they were "rediscovered" through such twentieth-century scholars as J. R. Geiselmann and Yves Congar. They were to influence twentieth-century ecclesiology profoundly. Certainly, for example, the great Cardinal Yves Congar, OP (1904-1995), perhaps the most accomplished ecclesiologist of the twentieth century, said in a number of interviews he gave late in life that Möhler had a profound impact on his own ecclesiological reflections. Equally, Geiselmann was studying Möhler for his own thinking on revelation and tradition, which were to have an impact on the *periti* of the Second Vatican Council, even copying out of Möhler's original notes from his canon law lectures in Tübingen before they were destroyed during the aerial bombardments of World War II.

Möhler's achievement in theology, then, might be said to be its very existence. As the principle of logic has it, *ab esse ad posse*. If theology, and indeed ecclesiology, *has been done* in the Möhler mode, it *can be* done in that way. And that brings us back to Cardinal Kasper's appreciation of a truly Catholic theology unfettered by scholasticism and seeking to read and relate to the signs of the times. Cardinal Kasper, of course, is the premier pupil of J. R. Geiselmann, who had prepared the German critical editions of Möhler's works, and so we may say that Möhler's influence has now reached the Roman curia.

On May 11, 1834, Thomas D. Acland, a friend of Newman, wrote to him: "Wiseman has desired me to draw your attention to a German work by Möhler, on Athanasius and his times. Very Roman Catholic, I believe."[25] On March 8, 1843, Newman wrote to a friend, Mary Holmes, who had asked him about Möhler: "Möhler's works are, I believe, very interesting."[26] Though it is debated whether Newman ever read Möhler himself, his thought was undoubtedly known to Newman—both Möhler's thinking on the development of doctrine and his ecclesiology. The work of Möhler provided reading for another important nineteenth-century figure, the American Isaac Hecker. Well before Hecker made his way into the Catholic Church he had been reading Möhler. Both Newman and Hecker await consideration in later chapters.

Bibliography

Himes, Michael J. *Ongoing Incarnation: Johann Adam Möhler and the Beginnings of Modern Ecclesiology*. New York: Crossroad, 1997.

Möhler, Johann Adam. *Unity in the Church, or the Principle of Catholicism Presented in the Church Fathers of the First Three Centuries*. Edited and translated by Peter C. Erb. Washington, DC: Catholic University of America Press, 1996.

————. *Symbolism: Exposition of the Doctrinal Difficulties between Catholics and Protestants as Evidenced by Their Symbolical Writings*. Introduction by Michael J. Himes. New York: Crossroad, 1997.

Savon, Herve. *Johann Adam Möhler, The Father of Modern Theology*. Glen Rock, NJ: Paulist Press, 1966.

Notes

1. Alexander Dru, *The Contribution of German Catholicism* (New York: Hawthorn Books, 1963), 60–61.

2. Walter Kasper, *Theology and Church* (New York: Crossroad, 1989), 5.

3. Herve Savon, *Johann Adam Möhler, The Father of Modern Theology* (Glen Rock, NJ: Paulist Press, 1966), 19.

4. Ibid., 20.

5. Peter C. Erb, "Introduction," in Johann Adam Möhler, *Unity in the Church, or the Principle of Catholicism Presented in the Spirit of the Church Fathers of the First Three Centuries,* ed. and trans. Peter C. Erb (Washington, DC: Catholic University of America Press, 1996), 23.

6. Erb, "Introduction," 21.

7. Cited in Erb, "Introduction," 28–29.

8. Savon, *Johann Adam Möhler,* 117.

9. Ibid., 27.

10. Ibid., 29.

11. Michael J. Himes, "The Development of Ecclesiology: Modernity to the Twentieth Century," in *The Gift of the Church,* ed. Peter C. Phan (Collegeville, MN: Liturgical Press, 2000), 56.

12. Cited in Erb, "Introduction," 1.

13. Möhler, *Unity in the Church,* 143.

14. Ibid., 153.

15. Ibid., 111.

16. Erb, "Introduction," 12.

17. Möhler, *Unity in the Church,* 179–80.

18. Dennis M. Doyle, "Möhler, Schleiermacher and the Roots of Communion Ecclesiology," *Theological Studies* 57 (1996): 471.

19. Möhler, *Unity in the Church,* 93.

20. Ibid., 252.

21. Savon, *Johann Adam Möhler,* 71.

22. Bradford E. Hinze, "The Holy Spirit and the Catholic Tradition: The Legacy of Johann Adam Möhler," in *The Legacy of the Tübingen School,* ed. Donald J. Dietrich and Michael J. Himes (New York: Crossroad, 1997), 77.

23. Johann Adam Möhler, *Symbolism: Exposition of the Doctrinal Difficulties between Catholics and Protestants as Evidenced by Their Symbolical Writings,* introduction by Michael J. Himes (New York: Crossroad, 1997), 259.

24. Dennis Doyle, *Communion Ecclesiology* (Maryknoll, NY: Orbis Books, 2000), 37.

JOHANN ADAM MÖHLER (1796–1838)

25. Anne Mozley, ed., *Letters and Correspondence of John Henry Newman During His Life in the English Church* (London: Longmans Green, 1891), 2:40.

26. Unpublished letter, cited in Günter Biemer, "A Vivified Church: Common Structures in the Ecclesiology of Johann Adam Möhler and John Henry Newman," in *Sinnsuche und Lebenswenden: Gewissen also Praxis nach John Henry Newman,* ed. Günter Biemer et al. (Frankfurt: Peter Lang, 1998), 245.

2
POPE PIUS IX (1792–1878)

Pius was the first pope to identify himself wholeheartedly with ultramontanism, i.e., the tendency to centralize authority in church government and doctrine in the Holy See.

—John N. D. Kelly[1]

Pope Gregory XVI to some extent distrusted Cardinal Giovanni Maria Mastai-Ferretti and said that even Mastai-Ferretti's cats were liberals. Mastai-Ferretti was elected pope as Gregory's successor in 1846, taking the name of Pius IX, and served the church in that capacity until his death in 1878. He is known in history popularly as Pio Nono.

Ordained a priest in 1819, he accompanied Monsignor Giovanni Muzi, apostolic delegate to Chile and Peru from 1823 to 1825. This experience stimulated his interest in the missions. After his return he showed no interest in pursuing a diplomatic career. He became archbishop of Spoleto in 1827, transferred to Imola in 1832 and was made cardinal in 1840. While in Imola, Mastai-Ferretti was very popular with the poor, so much so that he was constantly reduced too penury. He was elected pope in 1846, as Pius IX.

No one disagreed with the universally acknowledged fact that Pio Nono was a most charming man. Eamon Duffy writes: "He was genial, unpretentious, wreathed in clouds of snuff, always laughing."[2] Even his critics had to admit that he was most likable. "This tribute from Newman, who had no great opinion of his sagacity, seems to have been thoroughly deserved: "His personal presence was of a kind that no one could withstand....

18

The main cause of his popularity was the magic of his presence....His uncompromising faith, his courage, the graceful mingling in him of the human and the divine, the humour, the wit, the playfulness with which he tempered his severity, his naturalness, and then his true eloquence."[3]

Apparently, his sense of fun virtually knew no bounds. On one occasion, a number of Anglican clergymen were visiting Rome and had asked for his blessing. Pius pronounced over them, with humor, the prayer for the blessing of incense: "May you be blessed by Him in whose honor you are to be burned."[4] Pius moved with ease in the company of women, and it was rumored that there had been some sexual irregularity when he was younger, though as Eamon Duffy acknowledges this would "not necessarily (have been) damaging in Italian opinion."[5] An admirer of Queen Victoria, who sent him a personal letter of sympathy in 1848 at the time of the revolution that took him into exile, he seems to have considered himself a progressive Victorian.[6]

As a thinker, Pius was no intellectual. Odo Russell, the British ambassador to the Holy See and a man who was genuinely fond of Pius, commented on his "amiable but weak mind."[7] In this regard, advisers became all-important, but here too Pius was not blessed with great success. He placed too much faith and trust, for example, in Monsignor George Talbot, a converted Anglican priest. Talbot was unstable and reactionary. He sowed suspicions in the pope's mind about the orthodoxy and fidelity of Newman. Duffy describes the man in devastating terms: "He was certainly devious, feline, wreathed in intrigue, his view of the world and the Church a perpetual game of cowboys and Indians, heroes and villains."[8] In 1868 Talbot was removed from the Roman curia and placed in a mental institution near Paris, where he died in 1886.

While George Talbot was papal chamberlain, Cardinal Giacomo Antonelli was secretary of state. He was an ecclesiastical careerist who never moved beyond diaconate toward priesthood. Detailed and lurid accounts of Antonelli's sex life abound, making it exceedingly difficult to know what to believe.[9] Perhaps it is best to say with Duffy that the cardinal "practiced celibacy only episodically."[10] What is not in doubt is that Antonelli used his powerful office to promote his family to such an extent that he was accused of replacing the nepotism of popes with the nepotism of the secretary of state. Three of his brothers were given well-paying jobs in the papal civil service, and all were made papal counts. At the same time, Antonelli attended Mass daily, received communion once a week, and dispersed large amounts of money to various charities. One of the recipients of Antonelli's charity was Don Giovanni Bosco, now St. John Bosco, in his work for abandoned children. Owen Chadwick sums up Antonelli in these words: "He had not been ordained to be priestly, he was ordained because that opened a career."[11]

The Unification of Italy

Italy was not the unified state we know today, but was divided up into various kingdoms and principalities, including the Papal States. A movement was under way in the mid-nineteenth century to unite Italy under one leader, and for a time it seemed possible that that leader might be Pio Nono, a sort of president of a united Italy. Antonio Rosmini dreamed and hoped of such a possibility. Pius was perceived by many to be a reformer and a liberal. Soon after his election he embarked on a series of measures designed to improve the conditions in the Papal States. Almost immediately he declared an amnesty for former revolutionaries in the Papal States. He introduced railways and gas street lighting in Rome and put into place an agricultural institute to improve productivity and to help farmers make the most of their farms. He had the chains removed from the gates of the Jewish ghetto in Rome. Jews had been required to attend Christian sermons weekly, but Pius abolished this absurd requirement. Things were changing and changing fast in papal Italy. Pius ordered that insults against the Jews, fairly typical in the annual comedies of the Roman carnival, were to cease. The liberal sentiment exemplified by Pius finally led to the gates of the ghetto being burned down by the police of Rome. Frederic Ozanam, founder of the St. Vincent de Paul Society, described Pius in glowing terms: "The envoy sent by God to conclude the great business of the nineteenth century, the alliance of religion and liberty."[12] One Englishman writing to another in 1848 remarked: "A pretty state we are in altogether, with a Radical Pope teaching all Europe rebellion."[13]

The prospect, with whatever reality it had, came sharply to an end in the year 1848, the year of European revolutions, and the year in which the city of Rome itself fell to Italian revolutionaries. In that year Pius established an elected municipal government and agreed to a new constitution for the Papal States that included an elected chamber with the power to veto papal policy. As popular sentiment increasingly demanded the expulsion of Austria from Italy, however, Pius was called upon to give his leadership to this move. His response was to affirm that he would not send troops against a Catholic nation and to invite Italians to return to their established princes and abandon the notion of a united and federal Italy under his proposed leadership. Duffy describes what happened: "Overnight, from being the most popular man in Italy, he became the most hated."[14] In November of 1848 his prime minister, Pellegrino Rossi, was murdered, and in the same month Pio Nono had to escape from the city dressed as a simple priest. Rome was in revolt. From the safe position of Gaeta, in Naples, the pope called upon the Catholic powers of Europe to restore him. In July 1849, French troops took Rome, and Pius returned in 1850. Duffy writes: "He never recovered from his exile of 1848, and for the rest of his life remained convinced that political concessions to democracy merely fuelled the fires of revolution. The liberal honeymoon was over."[15] For the next two decades the pope depended on the presence of French and Austrian troops to maintain his position in the Papal States.

Reaction to European Liberalism

Liberalism is a notoriously slippery word, but we may take our point of departure for its definition from Alec Vidler: "Broadly speaking, in the nineteenth century Liberals were those people who were in favour of the new kind of state and society that had issued from the (French) Revolution."[16] "Freedom, equality, brotherhood" had been the cry of the French Revolution, and liberals were those who wanted to see that cry echoed in every aspect of society. Liberalism referred to those who espoused constitutional and representative governments, who favored religious toleration, and who advocated the separation of church and state. These ideas were commonplace in Europe and in the United States of America and were daily gaining ground, also among many Catholics. Although it is dangerous to make grand and general descriptions, it is probably fair to say that political liberalism marked France and parts of Italy especially, while a more intellectual liberalism was characteristic of England and Germany.

Pius was deeply opposed to religious toleration. He came out against, for example, the modest degree of tolerance shown toward Protestant worship by the Spanish government. He took issue with the Grand Duke of Tuscany, who permitted Jews to attend the university. In Italy the center of liberalism was undoubtedly Turin in Piedmont. Its king, Victor Emmanuel II, with his prime minister, Count Cavour, continued to promote the cause of Italian unification, especially against the Austrian presence. A policy hostile to the church was pursued in Piedmont. For example, in 1854, almost all monasteries and convents were suppressed, except for some nursing and teaching congregations. In 1860 the Legations and the Marches of Ancona, both within the Papal States, were taken by Piedmont. A small residual strip of land on the west coast of Italy was all that remained of the Papal States. Defense forces from devout Catholics came together from all over

Europe on behalf of the pope. French, Spanish, Portuguese, Polish, Irish—all rallied to the papal side. The Irish brigade was under the command of one Major O'Reilly. Duffy notes wittily that the pope was initially doubtful about the Irish contingent in these defense forces "because he feared the effects on Irishmen of the ready availability of cheap Italian wine."[17] From the perspective of Pio Nono, the entire situation in Italy had a rather apocalyptic feel to it. On the one hand was liberal Piedmont representing the forces of evil, and, on the other, himself leading the legions of God.[18]

To Pio Nono's struggle with liberalism we must add the Mortara episode.[19] Edgardo Mortara was a Jewish boy whose family lived in Bologna, which was within the Papal States. When he was still only one, Edgardo became seriously ill, and a Christian servant in the Mortara household baptized him secretly, fearing that the child would die without the benefit of the sacrament. The story of the secret baptism broke, and the Inquisition moved in. Since Edgardo was now technically a Christian, and since the law forbade Christians to be brought up as Jews, the now six-year-old was taken from his parents and put under the direct protection of the pope himself. There was, as one might expect, an uproar throughout the world, but Pius was deaf to all pleas to return the child to his parents. Without intending it, the pope's involvement drew the church into disrepute at the popular level. Duffy writes of the affair: "[Pius] made a pet of Edgardo, escorting him into public audiences, playing hide and seek with him under his cloak."[20] The boy never was returned to his parents, eventually became a priest, and lived into the 1930s. "His case was both a human tragedy and a demonstration of the gulf which had opened up between the thought-world of the papacy, and the secular liberal values which were now the moral currency of Europe, even for many Catholics."[21] Duffy continues that Pius was not particularly anti-Semitic, "except in the tragically general sense in which most Christians were anti-Semitic."[22]

Pius distanced himself from every aspect of liberalism in 1864 with the publication of two documents: the encyclical letter *Quanta Cura* and the *Syllabus of Errors*. The immediate catalyst for the encyclical was a Catholic congress held at Malines, Belgium, in 1863. At this congress, Montalembert, a French Catholic liberal politician whose constant dream was the reconciliation of Catholicism and the modern world, strongly encouraged a reconciliation between the church and democracy. His speech was later published under the title "A Free Church in a Free State." In his speech Montalembert said that too many Catholics associated the church with the *ancien régime,* and, while the *ancien régime* may have had its merits, it had one major demerit—it was dead. He advocated the church's universal acceptance of democracy.[23] Montalembert's views were not welcomed in Rome. Pius's secretary of state, Cardinal Antonelli, rebuked Montalembert and the archbishop of Malines in 1864, and in December of that year, on the tenth anniversary of the definition of the Immaculate Conception, *Quanta Cura* was published. The *Syllabus,* a list of eighty condemned propositions based on the pope's previous statements and allocutions was a comprehensive condemnation of liberalism. Proposition 77 denied that non-Catholics should be free to practice their religion. Proposition 80 condemned the idea that "the Roman Pontiff can and should reconcile himself with progress, liberalism, and recent civilization." To be fair, the attention of the *Syllabus of Errors* immediately stemmed from and was focused on the Italian liberals who were bent on the suppression of the temporal power of the papacy and the unification of Italy. It had in mind the policies of the Piedmontese government against the church. But it did not sound like that publicly. Taken as a whole and without contextual nuance, "[i]t seemed that the pope had declared war on modern society in all its aspects."[24]

Alec Vidler maintains, and rightly, that it is only fair to admit that Pius near the end of his life recognized his limitations in this regard and confessed: "I hope my successor will be as much attached to the Church as I have been and will have as keen a desire to do good: beyond that, I can see that everything has changed; my system and my policies have had their day, but I am too old to change my course; that will be the task of my successor."[25]

Ultramontanism

Literally, the term *ultramontanism* means "beyond the mountains" and refers to an interpretation of the Christian reality that is totally centered on the reality of the papacy. Pio Nono's reign witnessed the rapid development and perhaps the climax of ultramontanism. Alec Vidler comments: "The mystique about the Holy Father, and what often seems an unwholesome adulation of his person, date from Pius IX."[26] In some quarters the pope was spoken of as "the vice-God of humanity." One French ultramontane bishop maintained that the pope was the continuation of the incarnate Word. The Jesuit review *Civiltà Cattolica* put it about that when the pope meditated God was thinking in him. Extreme language, indeed. At the popular level, Catholics all over the world had pictures of Pius in their homes, and steamships and railways enabled relatively easy frequent pilgrimage to Rome. Add to this the emergence of foreign correspondents for national newspapers, and Pius became, in the words of Jesuit historian John W. O'Malley, "the first papal mega-star."[27] Needless to say, not all Catholics were ultramontane in outlook. Speaking of an excessive devotion to the person of the pope, the archbishop of Rheims stated that it was "an idolatry of the papacy."[28]

From the perspective of ultramontanism, anything less than a complete identification with and endorsement of the pope was less than Catholic and was immediately suspect. Though the ultramontane perspective at Vatican I will be examined in more detail later, suffice it to say that Pius encouraged this point of view. He threatened bishops who were inclined to disagree with the definition of infallibility, and he raised to the episcopate men who were strongly ultramontane. One historian captures the mood in these words: "(Pius) used the apostolic nuncios as watchdogs to keep the bishops in line; recalcitrants were sometimes invited to a personal audience, which could be stormy."[29] This was also the time when national seminaries in Rome were encouraged, "where young seminarians…could imbibe the Roman spirit at its source."[30]

In similar fashion, in April 1870 Pius summoned the premier Vatican archivist, the Oratorian Augustin Theiner, a well-respected scholar, and charged him with providing documents to the anti-infallibilists, specifically Lord Acton. Pius considered them "enemies." In August of the same year Theiner was required to give up his keys to the archives. Although he was not actually dismissed and he did retain his title of prefect of the archives, he continued to work under the same difficult conditions as any ordinary scholar.[31]

Ultramontane or not, from the time of Pius IX there developed in the church a central place for the papacy in Catholic devotion and piety. A hymn that I was taught as a boy, the words for which were composed by Cardinal Nicholas Wiseman (1802–1865), expresses this piety clearly:

> Full in the panting heart of Rome,
> Beneath the Apostle's crowning dome,
> From pilgrim lips that kiss the ground,
> Breathes in all tongues one only sound,
> "God bless our Pope, the great, the good."

As a result of all these factors, a strong current of ultramontanism gained enormous ground not only among the clergy but among the ordinary people too.

The Papacy and the Episcopate

Pius introduced new hierarchies into England in 1850, and into the Netherlands in 1853. During his pontificate he created two hundred new bishoprics or apostolic vicariates. Duffy notes: "All this represented a massive growth of papal involvement and papal control in the local churches."[32] Bishops in the expanding church in the United Sates were appointed in Rome and developed a strong Rome-centeredness. Under Pius, missionary work, which he first undertook in 1823–1825 when he was in Chile and Peru, expanded throughout the world.

Pius and Popular Devotion

"Pius IX's real success was with the interior renewal of the Church, and he deserves credit for the magnificent leadership he gave in deepening its sense of piety and spirituality."[33] No account of Pio Nono would be complete if it did not turn attention to his promotion of devotion to the Sacred Heart and to the Blessed Virgin Mary. In 1856, Pius extended the Feast of the Sacred Heart to the universal church. "Through these devotions, through declaring Francis de Sales a doctor of the Church and through other means, Pius helped turn piety in a more heartfelt direction."[34] Some find it all too easy to pour scorn on such devotions as the Sacred Heart of Christ. Although much of the popular and widespread artwork associated with this devotion may be judged to be of a very poor quality, the very notion of the heart as a symbol of human love and commitment becomes a very powerful focus for expressing the divine love.[35] Not only piety but also the religious institutions of the church flourished during Pius's reign. During his time, the Society of Jesus almost doubled its membership, as did many other religious orders, for example, the Sulpicians, the Passionists, the Redemptorists, the Franciscans, and the

Dominicans. There were new foundations too: the Blessed Sacrament fathers, the so-called White fathers, and the Society of the Divine Word.

The demands for the definition of the dogma of the Immaculate Conception of Our Lady were being received at Rome long before Pio Nono. The demand had been heard increasingly in France since 1830, the year of the vision of Our Lady to St. Catherine Labouré in the Rue du Bac, Paris. In 1847, Giovanni Perrone, the leading theologian of the Roman schools, published a thesis to show that the doctrine of the Immaculate Conception could be defined. Pius appointed a commission to study the question, including the Jesuit theologian Passaglia. From exile in Gaeta in 1849, Pius issued the encyclical *Ubi Primum,* asking the advice and prayers of the worldwide episcopate. Of some six hundred episcopal replies, nine-tenths were entirely supportive of the dogma. The definition was drawn up by two Jesuits, Passaglia and Perrone, creating the popular but false impression that it was "an invention of the Jesuits." To offset this criticism, Pius invited a number of bishops at the last moment to modify the text of the definition. "We must accept this humiliation," he is reported to have said, "so that it won't be said that everything depended upon the Jesuits."[36]

The dogma of the Immaculate Conception was proclaimed on December 8, 1854. Although the doctrine was warmly received by most Catholics, there was those who did not accept it. One French priest, arguably mentally disturbed, who preached against the doctrine after the definition was suspended by the archbishop of Paris, Marie Dominique Auguste Sibour. The priest then stabbed the archbishop to death during a procession in a Paris church. Although Pius was in many ways following the movement of popular devotion in the proclamation of the Immaculate Conception, Owen Chadwick accurately states, "No previous Pope in eighteen centuries had made a definition of doctrine quite like this."[37]

Conclusion

Pio Nono died on February 7, 1878, the longest pontificate in the history of the church. With him from December 22, 1878, until his death was Henry Edward Manning, the ultramontane cardinal-archbishop of Westminster, who had stalwartly supported the pope since he first met him and asked his blessing as an Anglican Dean visiting Rome so many years before. When Pius's body was transferred to the Basilica of St. Lawrence-Outside-the-Walls in 1881, it was done at night because of the anticlericalism raging in the city. Even so it was unpleasant and the Roman mob threw mud from the Tiber at the coffin.

The whole strategy of Pio Nono's pontificate left its impress on the church for a century. While Pope Leo XIII and others attempted a more friendly and open attitude to the modern world, according to Alec Vidler, "there was no substantial change in the authoritarian pattern which [Pius] had canonized until the dramatic reign of John XXIII."[38] The papacy became authoritarian in style, and the church at large became defensive, and generally hostile to the "world."

Essentially, Vidler is right, but the beatification of both Pope John XXIII and Pope Pius IX on September 3, 2000, may help us to see that the Catholic Church is big enough to include in its communion those Christians who are more Pian in style, as well as those who are more Johannine. Although they will not agree on a number of issues, they agree in essentials and refuse to break communion. Pius's beatification may also serve to remind us, as Eamon Duffy has it, that "Christian sanctity takes many forms, is compatible with making a mess of things, and was not invented in the 1960s."[39]

Bibliography

Chadwick, Owen. *A History of the Popes 1830–1914.* Oxford: Clarendon Press, 1998.

Duffy, Eamon. *Saints and Sinners: A History of the Popes.* Rev. ed. New Haven/London: Yale University Press, 2001.

Hales, E. E. Y. *Pio Nono.* London: Eyre and Spottiswoode, 1954.

Notes

1. John N. D. Kelly, *The Oxford Dictionary of Popes* (New York/Oxford: Oxford University Press, 1986), 310.

2. Eamon Duffy, *Saints and Sinners: A History of the Popes,* rev. ed. (New Haven/London: Yale University Press, 2001), 293.

3. Cited from Alec R. Vidler, *The Church in an Age of Revolution,* rev. ed. (Harmondsworth: Penguin Books, 1974), 147.

4. Cited from Duffy, *Saints and Sinners,* 293.

5. Eamon Duffy, "It Takes All Sorts to Make a Saint," *The Tablet* (September 9, 2000): 1180.

6. E. E. Y. Hales, *Pio Nono* (London: Eyre & Spottiswoode, 1954), 129.

7. John W. O'Malley, SJ, "The Beatification of Pope Pius IX," *America* (August 26–September 2, 2000): 10.

8. Duffy, *Saints and Sinners,* 294.

9. See the careful first and last chapters in Frank J. Coppa, *Cardinal Giacomo Antonelli and Papal Politics in European Affairs* (Albany: State University of New York Press, 1990).

10. Duffy, "It Takes All Sorts to Make a Saint," 1180.

11. Owen Chadwick, *A History of the Popes 1830–1914* (Oxford: Clarendon Press, 1998), 94.

12. Roger Aubert, "Pius IX, Pope, Bl.," in *New Catholic Encyclopedia,* 2nd ed. (Detroit: Thomson/Gale in association with The Catholic University of America, 2003), 11:385; see also Hales, *Pio Nono,* 50–51.

13. Robert Wilberforce to J. B. Mozley, cited in Vidler, *Church in an Age of Revolution,* 148.

14. Duffy, *Saints and Sinners,* 288.

15. Ibid.

16. Vidler, *Church in an Age of Revolution,* 148.

17. Duffy, *Saints and Sinners,* 289.

18. Aubert writes: "To realists who tried to persuade him that sooner or later he must negotiate, Pius IX opposed a mystical confidence in divine providence, nourished by the conviction that the political convulsions in which he was implicated were only an episode *in the great battle between God and Satan, in which Satan's defeat was inevitable*" ("Pius IX, Pope, Bl.," 385; emphasis added).

19. See David I. Kertzer, *The Kidnapping of Edgardo Mortara* (New York: Knopf, 1997).

20. Duffy, *Saints and Sinners,* 289.

21. Ibid., 290.

22. Duffy, "It Takes All Sorts to Make a Saint," 1181.

23. See Chadwick, *History of the Popes 1830–1914,* 170–72.

24. Vidler, *Church in an Age of Revolution,* 151.

25. Cited from Vidler, *Church in an Age of Revolution,* 153.

26. Vidler, *Church in an Age of Revolution,* 153.

27. O'Malley, "Beatification of Pope Pius IX," 8; see also Chadwick, *History of the Popes,* 1830–1914, 113.

28. Vidler, *Church in an Age of Revolution,* 154.

29. Thomas Bokenkotter, *A Concise History of the Catholic Church,* revised and expanded edition (New York: Doubleday, 2004), 319.

30. Ibid.

31. Owen Chadwick, *Catholicism and History* (Cambridge: Cambridge University Press, 1978), 63–66. Chadwick's book offers many examples of Theiner's scholarly reputation. Eamon Duffy suggests mistakenly that Theiner was actually dismissed ("It Takes All Sorts to Make a Saint," 1181).

32. Duffy, *Saints and Sinners,* 304.

33. Bokenkotter, *Concise History of the Catholic Church,* 327.

34. O'Malley, "Beatification of Pope Pius IX," 8.

35. Consider, for example, the retrieval of this devotion by Karl Rahner, SJ.

36. Hales, *Pio Nono,* 148.

37. Chadwick, *History of the Popes 1830–1914,* 121.

38. Vidler, *Church in an Age of Revolution,* 156.

39. Duffy, "It Takes All Sorts to Make a Saint," 1182.

3
JOHN HENRY NEWMAN
(1801–1890)

Newman is far less dead, to me, than many of my contemporaries; and less dead, even, than Socrates for whom, in the day-dreams of my young youth, I thought it would be lovely to lay down my life....It was by way of Newman that I turned Roman Catholic. Not all the beheaded martyrs of Christendom, the ecstatic nuns of Europe, the five proofs of Aquinas, or the pamphlets of my Catholic acquaintance, provided anything like the answers that Newman did.

—Muriel Spark[1]

Conversion changed [Newman's] explicit allegiance and had immense consequences for the course of his life, but it did not overturn the pattern of his thinking. The continuities in his thought before and after conversion are in many ways more striking than the discontinuities.

—Patrick Allitt[2]

No account of the church or theology in the nineteenth century would be complete without attention to John Henry Newman, Anglican and Catholic, and Anglican and Catholic in such a way that the continuities between the one and the other are, in Patrick Allitt's words, "more striking than the discontinuities." The life and commitment of John Henry Cardinal Newman demonstrate the best of what it means to be a Catholic Christian in both ecclesial traditions. The immediate difficulty is how to deal with the enormous amount of data and interpretations. There is an entire Newman industry with detailed studies on every part of his life and thought. Few theological authors have provided us with such rich autobiographical data as Newman—his *Apologia pro Vita Sua,* his diaries, and his letters are all now available in print. When it comes to a basic introduction to Newman, selection of material becomes, therefore, all-important. Thus, there are three parts to this chapter, under the headings "Newman, Man of the University," "Newman, Man of the Church," and "Newman the Man." These admittedly artificial divisions will enable us to see the continuities and the discontinuities to some extent, but more importantly, will make Newman more manageable. One might wonder, however, why attention is given to "Newman the man." Why not be content with an elucidation of Newman's contribution to and understanding of the university and the church? Why probe into his humanity, his character traits, his person? One might be the greatest scholar in the world, the most devout Christian in the church, but somehow one's real and substantive contribution seems to shine through simply and with conviction in one's person, in how one talks, relates, deals with problems, flourishes in friendships and commitments. Newman was a very fine man—distinguished, yes; famous, undoubtedly. But he was also a very good man, a very ordinary man in so many ways, a man with whom one can easily identify.

Brief Biographical Sketch

Newman's life spans the whole of the nineteenth century, but it was a difficult life in so many ways. Louis Bouyer, the French Oratorian, says of Newman: "It is not an exaggeration to say that Newman was a little or not at all understood by his contemporaries."[3] This is one of the continuities in Newman. Bouyer is referring to the fact that when Newman left the Church of England, his leaving was little understood by many of his fellows in the Oxford Movement, and his leaving took many with him to Rome. Equally, however, he was not entirely accepted by many Catholics, who found his way of doing theology and some of his ideas curiously suspect, at least until the time of Pope Leo XIII, who undid much of this suspicion by making Newman a cardinal.

John Henry Newman, the eldest of six children, was born in London on February 21, 1801, and he died in Birmingham on August 11, 1890. Here are noted the main essentials of his life as a prelude to a closer examination of his person and meaning. He attended a private boarding school at Ealing and was a star pupil, excelling in the Greek and Latin classics but demonstrating considerable skill in music, the violin being his instrument. He set up a newspaper in the school, in which he did most of the writing. One contribution interestingly comes from a certain John Quincy Adams, later president of the United States, whose son was at the school. Newman was not much of a sportsman, but he liked to swim—his schoolboy diary is full of entries of bathing in the river. He was also very religious, and at the age of sixteen Newman tells us that he underwent a conversion, from "an unbelieving boy" to a "Christian." This was partly due to an evangelical master at his school.[4]

The evangelical milieu of the school also had its influence on John Henry's younger brother, Francis Newman (1805–1897). They were very different. Indeed, Basil Willey describes the differences in this way:

> In the history of nineteenth century English thought there is no story more striking, or more full of moral significance, than that of the divergent courses of the brothers Newman. It is as if two rivers, taking their rise in the same dividing range, should yet be deflected by some minute irregularity of level, so that one pours its waters into the Mediterranean, the other into the German Ocean.[5]

The analogy is particularly apt. Newman became a Mediterranean Catholic, and Francis, after a spell of evangelical fervor that took him as a missionary to Baghdad, became something of a northern European rationalist. Willey does not speak of the third Newman brother, Charles, who adds to the complexity of this family. But more about Charles Newman later.

After boarding school, Newman went up to Trinity College, Oxford, in 1817. While he clearly enjoyed his studies, he found his first two years in university difficult. The late Meriol Trevor, in her splendid biography of Newman, expresses Newman's difficulties in her own inimitable way: "He was two years younger than most men of his year and came from a very different background. Trinity was certainly gentlemanlike—nobody did much work and everybody drank a lot of wine."[6] Francis followed him to Oxford, to Worcester College, and John considered him a superior Greek scholar.

After his studies, John was ordained a deacon of the Church of England in 1824 and a priest the following year. Stephen Dessain, the premier Newman scholar of his generation, tells us that after ordination "[Newman] wrote a sentence which gives the key to all his subsequent history: 'I have the responsibility of souls on me to the day of my death.'"[7] He remained in Oxford from 1817 to 1846 in various capacities: as a fellow of Oriel College, as a college tutor, as vicar of the university church of St. Mary the Virgin, and at his community of Littlemore, but the care of souls remained central to everything he did.

In 1832 Newman went on a Mediterranean trip with his friend Richard Hurrell Froude, the high Anglican who had introduced him to the full doctrine of the sacraments, the eucharistic presence of Christ, and devotion to Mary, Mother of God. Froude had tuberculosis and his archdeacon-father hoped that this trip would be beneficial for his health. Newman joined them. "The whole of this journey was to be for Newman a voyage into his own soul, ending with a death and resurrection in Sicily."[8] When the Froudes were ready to return to England, Newman decided to stay, against their advice, and to explore

Sicily for himself. He became seriously ill, the illness compounded about the initial doubts he had begun to feel about various aspects of his own Anglican Church.

> As I lay in bed the first day, many thoughts came over me. I felt God was fighting against me—and felt at last I knew why—it was for self-will....Yet I felt and kept saying to myself "I have not sinned against the light."[9]

Though he felt he had not sinned against the light, he sensed a keen opposition between his own self-will and what God wanted from him. It was on his delayed return to England that Newman composed one of his most famous pieces of verse, "Lead Kindly Light":

> Lead, kindly Light, amid the encircling gloom,
>   lead Thou me on.
> The night is dark and I am far from home,
>   lead Thou me on.
> Keep Thou my feet; I do not ask to see
> the distant scene; one step enough for me.

On the very same day that John arrived back in England from Sicily, Francis arrived back from his ill-starred mission to Baghdad. Coincident with John's return to England was the birth of the Oxford Movement in the Church of England, when John Keble preached his famous Assizes Sermon on "National Apostasy." The Oxford Movement was a complex phenomenon, but "essentially, the movement was the rediscovery of the Church as an autonomous community, organically one with the first disciples of Christ."[10] To so many outsiders, however, the movement was seen as a Romanizing of the Church of England, as a selling out of the Reformation. Through his preaching and teaching and writing Newman was thought of as a "crypto-Romanist" by his peers in the church. Though he professed obedience to his own Anglican bishop, the bishop of Oxford, it did not look like that to his critics. Newman's theological views were becoming more and more Roman Catholic, despite his allegiance to his bishop. Meriol Trevor rightly comments that Newman's influence, both as an Anglican and as a Catholic, tended to intimidate bishops of either church. She writes: "Newman's personal influence was to make him, all his life, far more important than any bishop, Anglican or Catholic, under whom he acted as a simple clergyman. It was like having an unexploded bomb in your diocese."[11] This emerges especially from some of the *Tracts for the Times* that Newman authored. For example, in Tract 1 he wrote: "Black event as it would be for the country, yet...we could not wish [the bishops] a more blessed termination of their course than the spoiling of their goods and martyrdom."[12] Or again, in the final and famous Tract 90 on the Anglican Thirty-nine Articles, in which Newman suggested that there were no barriers in the Articles to the acceptance of Roman Catholic doctrine. The spoiling of one's goods and the prospect of martyrdom may be seen as a sort of rhetorical flourish, not to be taken too seriously, but the acceptance of Roman Catholic doctrine? Now the bomb was ready to explode! The reactions to Tract 90 ranged "from thinking it was an attempt to join England with Rome, to holding it to be a dastardly example of sophistry."[13] It was the end of the Tracts, and although still 1841, it was the end for Newman as an Anglican.

After a long and difficult personal struggle, Newman entered the Catholic Church on October 8, 1845, being conditionally baptized and received by the Italian Passionist priest Blessed Dominic Barberi. He returned briefly to Oxford in 1846 to pack his things. A number of his friends came to see him, to make their farewells: "Pusey last of all, late at night. Newman left Oxford next morning at half-past eight and did not see it again, except from the train, for thirty-two years."[14] All considered, he had spent twenty-five years in his beloved Oxford, and he would not see Edward Bouverie Pusey, the Regius Professor of Hebrew and one of his closest friends again until they were both old men. That same year, 1846, saw

Francis appointed professor of Latin at University College London, a post he was to hold until 1863.

In 1847 John was ordained a Catholic priest in Rome and joined the Oratory of St. Philip Neri with some companions. At the end of that year he returned to England, and in 1848 established an English Oratory in Maryvale, at that time just outside Birmingham. The year 1849 saw the oratory moved to a former gin distillery in downtown Birmingham, and finally in 1852 to its present site in Edgbaston, Birmingham.

Throughout his life Newman was a writer. He wrote theological works mainly, but in 1852 he gave a series of lectures in Dublin, Ireland, on university education that saw life in print as *The Idea of a University*. This conceptual blueprint was to take living flesh as the Catholic University of Ireland to which Newman was appointed as rector in 1854. Superficially, it may seem strange to appoint an Englishman as rector of a Catholic university in Ireland in the mid-nineteenth century, a time when Irish nationalism was growing. But who would have seemed more suitable than the distinguished Oxford convert? He remained in that position until 1857, when, for both personal and ecclesiastical reasons, he resigned. During this period he was constantly crossing St. George's Channel between England and Ireland, dividing his time between the Birmingham Oratory of which he was the founding father, and the Catholic University of Ireland as rector.

During the 1860s Newman found himself in a difficult position. Many, especially Anglican converts like Henry Edward Manning, archbishop of Westminster, were pushing for a definition of papal infallibility, but a very wide-ranging definition. One Newman expert describes the situation accurately: "A violent campaign seemed to turn the Pope into an oracle independent of the Church."[15] Newman disagreed. Though he accepted the notion of papal infallibility, he felt it would be widely misunderstood and that it was not really necessary. This rendered him even further suspect in an English church whose leadership was very ultramontane at the time. Papal infallibility was defined at the First Vatican Council in 1870, the year in which Newman published *An Essay in Aid of a Grammar of Assent.* The cloud of suspicion under which Newman lived was lifted when he was made a cardinal by Pope Leo XIII in 1879. "'My cardinal,' declared Leo proudly. 'It was not easy...they said he was too liberal.'"[16] This act vindicated him against those extremist critics who, especially in respect of papal infallibility, had regarded him as unsound or less than fully Catholic.

When Newman died in 1890, the end was very simple. "There were no last words. Newman went out of this world as quickly and quietly as he went in and out of the rooms in it, surprising people who had expected a more formal presence."[17] After his death, however, hundreds filed past his coffin in the Oratory in Birmingham, and thousands lined the route to his final resting place at Rednal, just south of the city. The *Daily News* at his death said that "thousands know that they have lost one in whom their faith rested, one who was a living incarnation of the defensibility of faith, one on whose authority they could quote an argument to sustain them in their acceptance of the unseen."[18]

Newman, Man of the University

In a memorandum written in 1863 Newman wrote, "From first to last...education has been my line."[19] Newman always believed in the central importance of thinking for oneself, trying out ideas, being open to the critical and corrective judgments of others. In his *Idea of a University,* Newman wrote:

> Great minds need elbow-room, not indeed in the domain of faith, but of thought. And so indeed do lesser minds, and all minds....Every human system, every human writer, is open to just criticism. Make him shut up his portfolio; good! And then perhaps you lose what, on the whole and in spite of incidental

mistakes, would have been one of the ablest defenses of Revealed Truth (directly or indirectly according to his subject) ever given to the world.[20]

Thinking for yourself, however, did not mean for him either thinking by yourself or thinking that all thinking was equally valuable. He was opposed to both solipsism—that the discrete individual somehow is the criterion of all truth—and to what he called liberalism. Newman was consistently opposed to liberalism, but he meant by liberalism something quite precise. For Newman liberalism is the notion that one opinion is as good as another. He was open to new ideas, to the advancement of science as he understood it at the time. When Charles Darwin's *Origin of the Species* came out in 1859, shocking many devout Christians with its ideas of human evolution, the theory did not shock Newman. He wrote to a correspondent at the time that he was willing "to go the whole hog with Darwin."[21] In fact, Newman had a dynamic view of the universe long before many of his contemporaries. This dynamic perspective emerged especially from his studies of Christian antiquity.

Newman became immersed in the fathers of the church, in patristic theology. His close friend Edward Bouverie Pusey, who studied Hebrew and other Oriental languages as well as theology in Berlin, picked up for him folios of the fathers at a shilling each. Patristic studies had not yet come into their own in England. From his patristic studies Newman learned that change was essential to human flourishing, essential to the church. "The Church was not a changeless idea; it was a living community. Christ was one and the same, but the understanding of him must grow as the collective mind of the human race grows in the search for truth; the guidance of the Spirit was promised to, and mediated through, the united body. And St. Peter's successor was the divinely appointed center of unity."[22]

When eventually Newman found himself in Rome studying for the priesthood in the Catholic Church, the standard of university theology did not match the standard he had known in his beloved Oxford. According to his friend Ambrose St. John, he often fell asleep during lectures on moral and dogmatic theology. He was disappointed to find that theology was taught from second-rate manuals, and seldom from original sources. Few read St. Augustine or St. Thomas Aquinas. He referred to St. Thomas as "the champion of revealed truth," and when Pope Leo XIII later published an encyclical on Aquinas, Newman wrote to the pope to thank him for it. Nonetheless, Newman had nothing more than a layman's acquaintance with Aquinas. "He left Rome without having had any introduction to Thomistic philosophy or theology. His natural disinclination for metaphysics, added to this lack of any encouragement, left him all his life with no deep knowledge of Thomist metaphysics."[23]

When Newman was appointed rector of the Catholic University in Dublin, his ideal and his practice in the university shocked the then archbishop of Dublin, Cardinal Paul Cullen, who was himself responsible for Newman's appointment. Newman was all too aware of the many difficulties the new university faced both from church authorities and from external forces. But he did not give up. Newman gave the students very considerable freedom, both moral and intellectual—far too much, according to the archbishop. Newman established a science faculty and a school of medicine. Although the British government of the day refused to grant accreditation to the new university, which was seen as in opposition to the Queen's Colleges established in Belfast, Galway, and Cork, the Royal College of Surgeons in Dublin gave recognition to this new school of medicine, and it flourished from the beginning. Newman also appointed lay professors. Cardinal Cullen was opposed to this not least because the political views—that is, the republican views—of many of the Irish laity conflicted with his own. When Newman suggested to the bishops of Ireland who formed the board of governors of the university that it was necessary to appoint a vice-rector, they invited him to suggest one. When he suggested a layman and named him, silence ensued, and by the time Newman left, no one had been appointed. With both insight and wit, Meriol Trevor describes Newman's attitudes toward the student body:

> Newman expected the young men to keep horses and went riding with them himself, he encouraged music and debating societies and even, horror of horrors, supplied them with a club room and a billiard table, so that they could enjoy the favourite game of the day without resort to the places of entertainment in the town.[24]

Successive historians have emphasized the role of Newman in the university at the expense of that of Cardinal Cullen. The latter is seen more as an obstacle to the flourishing of Newman's project. It is true that there were real differences between the two men. The fact remains, however, that Cullen had recruited Newman and tried to keep him in Dublin. Cullen, of course, ever-cautious, moved much more slowly on issues facing the university than Newman would have wished. Newman's advocacy of lay professors and lay involvement was all fine and well, but Cullen was only too aware of the nationalistic and anti-British Young Irelanders, and of the volatile political climate.[25]

Newman has some fine things to say about the role of the teacher. He views the teacher, regardless of discipline, as a necessary intermediary in presenting the world of knowledge to the student. It is not simply the case that the teacher supplements what the student can learn from books and self-education. There is also what may best be described as "the personal presence of the teacher."[26] The text-person that is the teacher is every bit as important as the textbook. And so it comes as no surprise that teachers, in Newman's judgment, should exercise a certain personal-pastoral care for their students, especially in terms of their intellectual development. Contrary to many of his peers in Oxford at the time, Newman believed that tutors—in our terminology professors—should directly supervise students' work, and should take a real interest in the young men in their care. "This, in fact, was what tutorship became in Oxford."[27]

Newman was intellectually curious and thought that the university should likewise be a place of genuine intellectual curiosity. He loved visiting zoos until he was well over eighty. One companion of his to the Dublin zoo wrote in his diary: "To see Fr. Newman and [go] with him to the Zoological. His wonder at and speculation on the design and end of beasts; their ferocity; their odd ways; birds especially."[28]

Wide-ranging intellectual curiosity and religious devotion were not at odds for Newman. Here is his mission statement— as it would be called today—for the university:

> I wish the intellect to range with the utmost freedom and religion to enjoy an equal freedom; but what I am stipulating for is, that they should be found in one and the same place, and exemplified in the same persons....I want the same roof to contain both the intellectual and the moral discipline. Devotion is not a sort of finish given to the sciences; nor is science a sort of feather in the cap...an ornament and set-off to devotion. I want the intellectual layman to be religious and the devout ecclesiastic to be intellectual.[29]

Nor was Newman upset at intellectual differences between friends, among students, and even within the church. Writing to a critic who was also a friend from Oxford days, W. G. Ward, he said:

> I do not feel our differences to be such a trouble as you do; for such differences always have been, always will be in the Church; and Christians would have ceased to have spiritual and intellectual life if such differences did not exist. No human power can hinder it; nor, if it attempted it, could do more than make a solitude and

call it peace....Man cannot and God will not. He means such differences to be an exercise of charity. Of course, I wish as much as possible to agree with all my friends; but if, in spite of my utmost efforts, they go beyond me, or come short of me, I can't help it, and take it easy.[30]

Friends need not be clones, one of another, even in the most important areas of religious belief and expression.

Ultimately, Newman's idea of what a university education should produce is a gentleman. He had very strong and, it seems to me, entirely valid convictions about what a gentleman should be—and, were he alive today when access to university education is open to everyone, he would say also of a lady. Here is his description from *The Idea of the University:*

It is well to be a gentleman, it is well to have a cultivated intellect, a delicate taste, a candid, equitable, dispassionate mind, a noble and courteous bearing in the conduct of life; these are the connatural qualities of a large knowledge; they are the objects of a university; I am advocating, I shall illustrate and insist upon them....[31]

Two aspects of Newman's gentlemanly bearing ring out very clearly in this famous passage: a gentleman is to be intellectually cultivated, by which Newman means alive, aware, open to insight, pursuant of truth; he is to be courteous in his conduct. What a transformation of higher education would there be if both these qualities were bound indissolubly together!

Newman, Man of the Church

Perhaps most people think of Newman as Cardinal Newman, an eminent prince of the church. Newman was always a man of the church, church understood in the broadest possible sense. He was thoroughly an Anglican churchman before becoming a Roman Catholic churchman. When he became a Roman Catholic, he was forty-four. In this regard, Bishop Geoffrey Rowell, one of the premier contemporary historians of the Oxford Movement, points out:

> That simple fact is one we are apt to forget. His spirituality, his theological outlook, were already largely settled: men do not change drastically at such an age. In leaving the Church of England and joining the Church of Rome, he looked only for the more perfect realization of that faith by which he had tried to live as an Anglican.[32]

As a deacon in the Church of England, for example, this young intellectual threw himself into pastoral work. Meriol Trevor describes him:

> He started visiting, especially the sick, and keeping notes. Often he was taken in by pious talk and afterwards discovered that the person was a drunkard or had deserted his wife and children. From the dying he tried to elicit penitence and induce them to take the Sacrament which, as he was only a deacon, he could not administer himself. The case of a sick girl was very painful—"it is like a sword going through my heart." And there was a young married woman with consumption. "Her eyes looked at me with such meaning. I felt a thrill I cannot describe—it was like the gate of heaven." She died half an hour after he left, much comforted by his reading from St. John, though very ignorant of religion, as most of these poor people were.[33]

Pastoral care was never far from Newman's mind either in the Church of England or, as already noted, in the Catholic Church. He was constantly concerned with the care of souls. In the 1860s, the pompous Monsignor George Talbot wrote to Newman inviting him to preach in Rome to an audience ostensibly superior to anything he could find in the industrial maze that was Birmingham. Newman refused the invitation, writing the famous words, "Birmingham people have souls."

Newman was a great advocate of the laity in the church. The same Monsignor George Talbot in a famous article—which was also a caricature of Newman's views—written in a periodical called *The Rambler* described the role of the laity in the church as follows: "They wish to govern the Church in England by public opinion....What is the province of the laity? To hunt, to shoot, to entertain."[34] The laity should have nothing to do with ecclesiastical affairs. In a memorandum of some correspondence he had with the editor of *The Tablet,* a British Catholic weekly, Newman wrote: "The Church would look foolish without them."[35]

Newman avoided any sense of the church as sectarian, as exclusive, as isolated, as insular. Newman accepted the role of the papacy in the church as the final adjudicator in matters of doctrinal and moral teaching, but he objected to a sweeping application of infallibility to all the pronouncements of the pope and to the way in which the proponents of such sweeping infallibility accused those who disagreed of being unorthodox. During the time leading up to the declaration of papal infallibility, and in the light of the positions that emphasized the role of the pope out of all proportion to his real role in the church, Newman wrote: "Instead of aiming at being a worldwide power, we are shrinking into ourselves, narrowing the lines of communion, trembling at freedom of thought, and using the language of dismay and despair at the prospect before us, instead of, with the high spirits of the warrior, going out conquering and to conquer."[36] In point of fact, Newman had been invited to go to Rome for the First Vatican Council as an expert theologian, but he turned down the invitation on the grounds of age and health.

In terms of his own spiritual life, Newman had a constant and profound sense of God, of the immediate presence of God. This had been part of his experience since he was a boy. He wrote in his *Apologia pro Vita Sua*: "from a boy I had been led to consider that my Maker and I, His creature, were the two beings, luminously such, *in rerum natura.*"[37] Before God, the soul was, in his words, *sola cum Solo.*

> Common men see God at a distance....But the long practiced Christian, who, through God's mercy, has brought God's presence near to him, the elect of God, in whom the Blessed Spirit dwells, he does not look out of doors for the traces of God; he is moved by God dwelling in him, and needs not but act on instinct. I do not say there is any man altogether such, for this is angelic life; but it is the state of mind to which vigorous prayer and watching tend.[38]

This permeative sense that Newman had of God's presence, of the loving union of the soul with God, perhaps best understood as a mystical presence, as an "ontological mysticism,"[39] is finely described by Owen Chadwick: "God...was too instant for debate...God is simply there."[40]

The human person before God, *sola cum Solo,* is, however, not unconnected, not a discrete, atomistic individual, as it were. Newman has a relational view of the Christian person, embodied with others in Christ. Newman's understanding of the church is as communion, communion with the Triune God and communion with one another.

> This then is the special glory of the Christian Church, that its members do not depend merely on that which is visible, they are not mere stones of a building, piled one upon another, and bound together from without, but they are one and all the births and manifestations of one and the same unseen

spiritual principle or power, "living stones," internally connected, as branches from a tree, not as the parts of a heap. They are members of the Body of Christ.[41]

At least in some respects, his ecclesiology would resonate with the communion ecclesiology so much in fashion at this time.

Reading through the *Apologia pro Vita Sua* leads one to a further appreciation of Newman's communion ecclesiology. Charting his spiritual and theological development, he makes constant mention, with gratitude, of so many of his Anglican professors, priests, and peers—Walter Mayers of Pembroke College Oxford; Daniel Wilson, later to become bishop of Calcutta; Richard Whately, principal of Alban Hall Oxford and later archbishop of Dublin; William James and Edward Hawkins of Oriel College; John William Bowden, Richard Hurrell Froude, John Keble, Hugh Rose; William Palmer of Dublin and of Worcester College, and Edward Pusey of Christ Church. Their names and so many more unfold throughout the *Apologia*. Newman, now a Roman Catholic, recalls them graciously and with great kindness. This leads the historian Owen Chadwick to comment: "[Newman] taught [Catholics of the nineteenth century] to be more generous to other denominations, for no Roman Catholic priest had ever said thank you to the Anglicans with such heartfelt eloquence."[42]

Newman the Man

Man of the church, man of the university, in many ways an ideal man and an ideal priest, but also an ordinary man. Newman's very ordinariness is one of his most attractive features. A female admirer so showed her disappointment at Newman's ordinariness when she first met him that he wrote to her, "As for myself, you are not the first person who has been disappointed in me. Romantic people always will be. I am, in all my ways of going on, a very ordinary person."[43] There seems to have been little pretense in the man. He evinced so many ordinary characteristics of what it is to be human.

One of these was the common, perhaps universal experience of shame. Newman's father was not a great businessman. His business enterprises seldom were marked by success. There seems little doubt that this not only pained Newman but gave rise to shame. In later years when his sister, Harriett, told her husband, Tom Mozley, that her father had been a chief clerk in a London firm, this greatly annoyed Newman. Speaking to Mozley, he insisted that his father had been a partner. In point of fact, Newman was accurate, but one gets a sense that his desire for accuracy was in part fueled by a sense of shame at his father's commercial failures.[44]

He was extraordinarily introspective. In a manuscript he entitled *Memoranda,* which he marked as "personal and most private," covering the years 1804-1826, we are given glimpse after glimpse of Newman's introspection. The very production of the manuscript demonstrates this, as described by Sean O'Faolain: "He first wrote it in 1820–21; transcribed it in 1823, with additions; in 1840, with omissions; in 1872 he marked it 'to be partially and finally transcribed with great omissions and put aside for good'; but in 1874 he went at it again and cut out fifteen precious pages at the beginning."[45] We see it at work with *finesse* in the *Apologia pro Vita Sua.* Indeed, so much of Newman would be utterly opaque, unknown to us without his introspection. Such introversion and self-scrutiny, however, are not always blessings. Partly because of this introspection, Newman was able to cope with loss in this world. If the world and everything in it is only penultimately real—and Newman appears to have thought so—then loss can never finally be loss. Whether it is the loss of a childhood home, or of status, or in the death of friends, the conviction that there is no finality to it enables one better to deal with it. This is not to say that such loss is not keenly felt in its own way, but it is also fitted into a metaphysical scheme of things so that while it has its place, one is not overwhelmed by loss. Perhaps O'Faolain comes close to the truth when he remarks: "[Newman's] weakness was that he would always love most passionately when all was gone, always speak his love too late."[46] Many could identify with Newman in this regard.

Newman was a great reader of novels, and especially enjoyed the work of George Eliot and Anthony Trollope. He also loved music, a love that was born when he was at boarding school. In a letter to a friend he wrote: "I never wrote more than when I played the fiddle. I always sleep better after music. There must be some electric current passing from the strings through the fingers into the brain and down the spinal marrow. Perhaps thought is music."[47]

As an adolescent, Newman often clashed with his father, who thought he was becoming too religious for his own good. John recorded in his journal his father's words:

> Have a guard. You are encouraging a nervous and morbid sensibility, and irritability, which may be very serious. I know what it is myself, perfectly well. I know it is a disease of the mind. Religion, when carried too far, induces softness of the mind.[48]

His father's bias was wide of the mark. No one could accuse Newman of softness of the mind. His journal shows something of the man. He judges himself to be vain of his attainments, too conscious of social differences and class, and prone to bad temper and bad thoughts. When he became a Catholic in 1845, Newman wrote to his brother Francis to ask for his forgiveness for his bad temper and his cruelty when they were both young. In his much-edited *Memoranda* he wrote: "While with Frank at Oxford I have felt a spirit of desperate ill-temper, and sullen anger rush on me....So violent has this sometimes proved that I have quite trembled from head to foot and thought I should fall down under excess of agitation." Sean O'Faolain's description has the ring of accuracy: "[Newman] had a devilish temper, passions so ungovernable as to unman him, and a tongue that could clip a hedge."[49] While that may be so, it takes a big man to seek out forgiveness and effect reconciliation, and that was Newman's way. Frank visited John frequently, even into his eighties, in the Oratory in Birmingham. His other brother, Charles, born one year after John in 1802, was a trying and constant challenge to the Newman family throughout his life and an atheist; he was financially supported by both Frank and John. Charles lived in the Welsh town of Tenby for the last thirty to forty years of his life. John went to visit him in September 1882, sensing probably that the end could not be far off, but Charles would not see him. We can only imagine how Newman felt. But, when Charles died in 1884, it was John who paid for the funeral and the gravestone with the inscription, "O Lord, of your eternal mercy, do not despise the work of your hands."

It has been pointed out by A. N. Wilson that despite all his fine qualities as a priest, an intellectual, and a man, Newman did not have an obvious concern for the mass of ordinary people, or for the difficulties of their lives. Wilson contrasts Newman rather negatively with the Anglican theologian and social prophet Frederick Denison Maurice.

> While the Irish starved, [Newman] worried his mind about Augustine's controversy in the fourth century with the Donatists....Newman wrote from the middle of the slums of Birmingham as if he were an Oxford don...whereas Maurice was always engaged with realities external to himself. To this degree, Maurice—the Anglican professor hounded out of his theological chair for "heresy"—was in many ways more "Catholic" than Newman, the Roman convert who was to die a cardinal.[50]

Even acknowledging a degree of *animus* on Wilson's part toward Newman, there is something in what he says. Theology is always done somewhere, and if that place in no way affects the doer of theology, that is problematic, to say the least. Wilson goes on to point out that, when it was to his taste, Newman was very aware of contemporary events. He followed, for example, the Crimean War, cutting out from the *Times* the maps showing how the campaign was developing.[51] Undoubtedly, Newman must have felt compassion toward the famine-suffering Irish and toward the poor of Birmingham. It remains a legitimate question, however, why such factors did not seem to enter explicitly into his theological reflection.

Newman made and kept friends and was devoted to them. Monsignor Francis Davis of Oscott College drew an interesting and in some ways humorous contrast between Newman and St. Thomas Aquinas:

> "St. Thomas," wrote Chesterton, "was a huge heavy bull of a man, fat and slow and quiet; very mild and magnanimous but not very sociable, even apart from the humility of holiness; and abstracted, even apart from his occasional and carefully concealed experiences of trance and ecstasy." Newman, on the other hand, was thin and pale and slightly bent. He walked and talked rapidly, and spoke incessantly as he walked. He had large, lustrous eyes, seeming to pierce through both men and things. Though naturally shy on first acquaintance, he always found, and needed, friendship.[52]

After his friend Hurrell Froude died, Newman collected various essays of his for publication. While he was readying these essays, he wrote at the back of his diary for 1839 these words about Froude: "Farewell, most loved, so much missed, until that Day which shall make you, known to so few, manifest to all as you were."[53]

Perhaps his closest friend was Ambrose St. John, a young Anglican priest whom he met in 1843. After this first meeting, Newman wrote to their mutual friend Henry Wilberforce about St. John: "St. John goes tomorrow and I ought to thank you for letting me have the great pleasure of making his acquaintance. He wishes to pay me a longer visit—and I assure you I do." Meriol Trevor comments: "St. John's longer visit lasted the rest of his life."[54] Ambrose St. John had studied Hebrew and Syriac under Newman's friend Edward Pusey at Oxford. When Ambrose died quite suddenly at the age of sixty in 1875, Newman was almost paralyzed by grief; he was remembered as conducting the absolutions at the funeral Mass in the Oratory chapel with great difficulty. Meriol Trevor describes the scene, recorded by a boy in the congregation who was later to become an Oratorian: "As Newman was giving the absolutions to the dead, after the mass, he broke down and wept; the boy heard a strange noise all over the church and for a moment thought the people were laughing. But they were crying."[55] When Newman died, he was buried, according to his own wishes, in the same grave as Ambrose St. John at Rednal.

Newman never forgot his dead. "Nobody was forgotten; when they died, their names were stitched into the little anniversary book with its cross-stitched cover....Every week, nearly every day had its memorials and Littlemore parishioners jostled with Fellows of Oriel, Anglicans with Catholics, nuns, children, duchesses, theologians, doorkeepers—a long human litany."[56] He prayed for his sainted dead on the occasion of their anniversary. Friends were friends for life and into eternity.

Conclusion

Newman was an educator of educators, a university man. Newman was a churchman's churchman. And Newman was very human in the best sense of the word. Perhaps the most widely read of Newman's writings, at least in the nineteenth century, were his published sermons. Of course, academics took to his more philosophical and theological texts, but many ordinary people reaped great gains from his "ministry of the

Word." He was a master minister of the Word, and in the next chapter we shall see something of what this means.

Bibliography

Bouyer, Louis, CO. *Newman's Vision of Faith.* San Francisco: Ignatius Press, 1986.

Dulles, Avery R., SJ. *Newman.* London/New York: Continuum, 2002).

Trevor, Meriol. *Newman's Journey.* London: Collins, 1974.

Notes

1. Muriel Spark, Foreword, in *Realizations: Newman's Own Selections of His Sermons,* ed. Vincent F. Blehl, SJ (London, 1964), v–ix, cited in Sheridan Gilley, "Newman and the Convert Mind," in *Newman and Conversion,* ed. Ian Ker (Notre Dame, IN: University of Notre Dame Press, 1997), 6.

2. Patrick Allitt, *Catholic Converts: British and American Intellectuals Turn to Rome* (Ithaca/London: Cornell University Press, 1997), 3.

3. Louis Bouyer, CO, *Newman's Vision of Faith* (San Francisco: Ignatius Press, 1986), 9.

4. C. Stephen Dessain, CO, "Newman's Spirituality," in *English Spiritual Writers,* ed. Charles Davis (London: Burns & Oates, 1961), 139.

5. Basil Willey, *More Nineteenth Century Studies* (New York: Harper & Row, 1966), 11.

6. Meriol Trevor, *Newman's Journey* (London: Collins, 1974), 18.

7. C. Stephen Dessain, CO, "John Henry Newman: A Brief Biographical Sketch," in *Newman Studien X,* ed. Heinrich Fries and Werner Becker (Heroldsberg bei Nürnberg: Glock and Lutz, 1978), 22.

8. Trevor, *Newman's Journey,* 48.

9. Ibid., 51.

10. Ibid., 55.

11. Ibid., 76.

12. Marvin R. O'Connell, *The Oxford Conspirators: A History of the Movement 1833–1845* (London: Macmillan, 1969), 147.

13. Gary Lease, *Witness to the Faith: Cardinal Newman on the Teaching Authority of the Church* (Pittsburgh: Duquesne University Press, 1971), 69.

14. Trevor, *Newman's Journey,* 118.

15. Dessain, "John Henry Newman, A Brief Biographical Sketch," 24.

16. Cited in Adrian Hastings, "John Henry Newman," in *Key Thinkers in Christianity,* ed. Adrian Hastings, Alistair Mason, and High Pyper (New York/Oxford: Oxford University Press, 2003), 123.

17. Trevor, *Newman's Journey,* 265.

18. Quoted in H. Francis Davis, "Cardinal Newman," in Davis, *English Spiritual Writers,* 123.

19. John Henry Newman, *Autobiographical Writings* (London/New York: Sheed & Ward, 1956), 259.

20. John Henry Newman, *The Idea of a University,* ed. Ian T. Ker (New York/Oxford: Oxford University Press, 1976), 383–84.

21. Cited in Trevor, *Newman's Journey,* 111. See A. N. Wilson, *The Victorians* (New York/London: W. W. Norton, 2003), 100–101.

22. Trevor, *Newman's Journey,* 112.

23. H. Francis Davis, "Newman and Thomism," in *Newman Studien IV,* ed. Heinrich Fries and Werner Becker (Nürnberg: Glock and Lutz, 1957), 158.

24. Trevor, *Newman's Journey,* 162.

25. Colin Barr, *Paul Cullen, John Henry Newman and the Catholic University of Ireland, 1845-1865* (Leominster, UK: Gracewing, 2003).

26. D. G. Mulcahy, "Personal Influence, Discipline and Liberal Education in Cardinal Newman's Idea of a University," in *Newman Studien XI,* ed. Heinrich Fries, Werner Becker, and Guenter Biemer (Heroldsberg bei Nürnberg: Glock and Lutz, 1980), 152.

27. Trevor, *Newman's Journey,* 41.

28. Cited in Trevor, *Newman's Journey,* 164.

29. Cited in Trevor, *Newman's Journey,* 184.

30. Cited in Trevor, *Newman's Journey,* 225.

31. Newman, *Idea of a University,* ed. Ker, 110.

32. Geoffrey Rowell, "The Roots of Newman's 'Scriptural Holiness': Some Formative Influences on Newman's Spirituality," in Fries and Becker, *Newman Studien X,* 13.

33. Trevor, *Newman's Journey,* 29.

34. Cited in Trevor, *Newman's Journey,* 230.

35. Cited in Trevor, *Newman's Journey,* 194.

36. Cited in Trevor, *Newman's Journey,* 227.

37. John Henry Newman, *Apologia pro Vita Sua* (1890 ed.), 195, quoted in Davis, "Cardinal Newman," 127.

38. Newman, *Apologia pro Vita Sua,* quoted in Davis, "Cardinal Newman," 128.

39. Dessain, "Newman's Spirituality," 153.

40. Owen Chadwick, "John Henry Newman," in *Great Spirits 1000–2000,* ed. Selina O'Grady and John Wilkins (Mahwah, NJ: Paulist Press, 2002), 152.

41. John Henry Newman, *Parochial and Plain Sermons,* 4:169–71, cited in Dessain, "Newman's Spirituality," 148.

42. Chadwick, "John Henry Newman," 152.

43. Cited in Trevor, *Newman's Journey,* 100.

44. Sean O'Faolain, *Newman's Way* (New York: Devin-Adair, 1952), 6–7.

45. Ibid., 42.

46. Ibid., 55.

47. Cited in Trevor, *Newman's Journey,* 223.

48. Cited in Trevor, *Newman's Journey,* 22.

49. O'Faolain, *Newman's Way,* 64.

50. A. N. Wilson, *The Victorians* (New York/London: W. W. Norton, 2003), 149.

51. Ibid., 180.

52. Davis, *"Newman and Thomism,"* 157.

53. Cited in Trevor, *Newman's Journey,* 70.

54. Trevor, *Newman's Journey,* 99.

55. Ibid., 252.

56. Ibid., 263.

4

MASTER MINISTERS OF THE WORD: JOHN HENRY NEWMAN (1801–1890) AND GERARD MANLEY HOPKINS (1844–1889)

> *There is no question that the English sermon had never before and has never since attained such psychological intensity and subtlety as in Newman.*
>
> —Ian Ker[1]

> *Hopkins saw the poet's task as crafting poetic language in such a way that it sacramentally 'carried' the presence of Christ and encouraged the reception of this presence by the hearer.*
>
> —Philip A. Ballinger[2]

> *Newman is the only Catholic convert revolutionary in literature, with the possible exception of one figure he converted, Gerard Manley Hopkins, the fountainhead of modern English poetry.*
>
> —Sheridan Gilley[3]

In September 1866, a young, twenty-two-year-old Oxford undergraduate who was thinking about becoming a Catholic wrote the following letter to one of his closest friends:

Dr. Newman was most kind, I mean in the very best sense, for his manner is not that of solicitous kindness but genial and almost, so to speak, unserious. And if I may say so, he was so sensible. He asked questions which made it clear for me how to act; I will tell you presently what that is: he made me sure I was acting deliberately and wished to hear my arguments; when I had given them and said I could see no way out of them, he laughed and said, "Nor can I"....More than once when I offered to go he was good enough to make me stay talking."[4]

Dr. Newman is, of course, John Henry Newman, and the young student was Gerard Manley Hopkins. Hopkins had taken it into his head to write to Newman about his becoming a Catholic, and in October of the same year Newman received him into the church. Thus met two of the greatest word crafters in English of the nineteenth century. They have much to say to us about preaching the gospel in the twenty-first century. Both Newman and Hopkins, as Catholic priests, preached. Both wrote poetry. Although Newman may be characterized as the *preacher*-poet, Hopkins was the *poet*-preacher.

Newman: The Preacher-*Poet*

"The essential Newman was a preacher, and he followed the patristic tradition of making sermons the primary vehicle for theology."[5] Many associate Newman with his major theological works, for example, his *Essay in Aid of a Grammar of Assent* or his *Essay on the Development of Doctrine,* but these came later in his life. Long before these formal explorations in theology developed, Newman was a preacher. Newman's premier twentieth-century biographer, Ian Ker, writes:

> Newman may have thought that teaching was his real
> vocation and that his principal intellectual mission
> was the philosophical defense of religious belief, but
> the fact is that during at least the Anglican half of his
> life, he probably spent more time composing sermons
> than writing anything else.[6]

Very interesting language! Newman spent more time composing sermons than anything else. Today it is more "ecclesiastically correct" to speak of homilies than sermons. But what
about the language of "composition"? "Compose" probably
suggests someone who works in music, such as Beethoven,
Bach, or the Beatles. When Ian Ker uses the verb "compose" of
Newman's homiletic labor, he is trying to convey something of
the complexity and excitement of the task. Hours of preparation following upon years of philosophical and theological
foundation, finding just the right words so that you can, under
God's grace, make the right sound to resound in the hearts of
God's people. That's what "composing homilies" is about.
Many of Newman's sermons were published. At present, there
are thirty-six volumes of his collected works. Eight volumes are
given over to his *Parochial and Plain Sermons.* In point of fact,
however, these *Parochial and Plain Sermons* constitute only
about one-third of the pastoral sermons he wrote as an
Anglican. He published two volumes of sermons as a Catholic,
Sermons Addressed to Mixed Congregations and *Sermons Preached
on Various Occasions.* After his death, a small volume of sermons
was published as *Catholic Sermons of Cardinal Newman,* some
of which were preached in the Cathedral of St. Chad,
Birmingham. If the liturgy is primary theology, then the liturgical homily—what Newman called a "sermon"—surely must
feature as a normative and regular form of theology. This does
not mean, of course, that the homily is the place for heavy-duty
theological analysis. While the homily ought not to be a tract in
Christian doctrine or morality, it cannot be composed without
saturation in scripture, doctrine, moral theology, philosophy,

literature, and the multiple disciplines that go into the making of a preacher.

The Irish Benedictine Placid Murray believes that these *Plain and Parochial Sermons* of Newman "can hardly be surpassed as liturgical preaching."[7] For Newman, liturgical preaching was a means to an end, to draw the hearers into a fuller sense of communion with God, and to develop their sense of mission and witness in daily life. But, before we move more fully into Newman's understanding of liturgical preaching, Dom Placid Murray also reminds us that Newman considered preaching very broadly. This is what Newman wrote about preaching:

> In Scripture to preach is to do the work of an evangelist, is to teach, instruct, advise, encourage in all things pertaining to religion, in any way whatever. All education is a kind of preaching—all catechizing, all private conversation—all writing. In all things and at all times is a Christian minister preaching in the Scriptural sense of the word...and in all matters and pursuits of this world as truly, though not as directly as when engaged in religious subjects.[8]

There is a continuum among all education, catechizing, conversation, and writing. All Christians, in living out the witness of their baptism, are engaged in preaching, but there is a special commission to preach given to the ordained.

Newman offers his theology of this ordained ministry of preaching in an essay of 1855 entitled "University Preaching," which is included in his book *The Idea of a University*. For the sake of brevity and clarity we might summarize his views in three central points. First, the key idea and the central object of the preacher must be only one thing, "the spiritual good of the hearers." "As a marksman aims at the target and its bull's eye, and at nothing else, so the preacher must have a definite point before him, which he has to hit." Following St. Paul's line of thought in the First Letter to the Corinthians, Newman believes that questions of display and rhetoric and delivery and so forth are not the primary issue. The primary issue must be and must be only having one object and going after it, this "spiritual good." He cites St. Paul to the effect that "the kingdom of God is not in speech, but in power." "Talent, logic, learning, words, manner, voice, action, all are required for the perfection of a preacher; but 'one thing is necessary,'—an intense perception and appreciation of the end for which he preaches, and that is, to be the minister of some definite spiritual good to those who hear him." But the spiritual good must be something *definite,* not some vague or general spiritual good. To keep focus on this definite spiritual good, Newman says: "I would go the length of recommending a preacher to place a distinct categorical proposition before him, such as he can write down in a form of words, and to guide and limit his preparation by it, and to aim in all he says to bring it about, and nothing else." In other words, maintain one key central point in the homily. Newman is talking about focus and clear direction of thought. He is not opposed, of course, to the development of this one point, but such development as is undertaken should not detract from the one point that is being laid down. One must be able to see the wood and not just a number of trees, however fascinating such trees may be. With a definite object in mind, then, the preacher should

> study it well and thoroughly, and first make it his own, or else have already dwelt on it and mastered it, so as to be able to use it for the occasion from an habitual understanding of it; and that then he should employ himself, as the one business of his discourse, to bring home to others, and to leave deep within them, what he has, before he began to speak to them, brought home to himself. What he feels himself, and feels deeply, he has to make others feel deeply....[9]

The preacher must have brought the message, this one definite spiritual message home to himself before he shares it with his congregation.

Second, the preacher should be aware of his audience. There is no preaching in general for Newman. In *The Idea of a University,* he continues: "A hearer is included in the very idea of preaching; and we cannot determine how in detail we ought to preach, till we know whom we are to address." Newman recognizes, needless to say, that the great themes of the Christian tradition remain the same for everyone, but here he is advocating that the preacher know his audience, so that he can tailor what he has to say in such a fashion that it will be heard and understood. Newman provides an example from the New Testament to illustrate his point, St. Paul in the Acts of the Apostles:

> To the Jews he quotes the Old Testament; on the Areopagus, addressing the philosophers of Athens, he insists,—not indeed upon any recondite doctrine, contrariwise, upon the most elementary, the being and unity of God;—but he treats it with a learning and depth of thought, which the presence of that celebrated city naturally suggested."[10]

Preaching to worshiping Jews in their synagogues, and preaching to a philosophic club are different. They are different not because the philosophers are superior to the worshipers, nor because the worshipers are less wise than the philosophers, but *because the audience is different.* Essentially this is but a variation on Newman's key and opening point. Preaching should be aimed at a definite spiritual good to be effective, and if it is to achieve this definite spiritual good, the preacher needs to know his definite audience.

Third, is the issue of writing out a homily. This is disputed territory in the academy of homiletics! Should a preacher preach with a written text or not? Newman knows full well that there are different practices here, and he is respectful of practices that differ from his own, but he lays down quite clearly the importance of a written text. "These remarks, as far as they go, lead us to lay great stress on the preparation of a sermon, as amounting in fact to composition, even in writing, and *in extenso.*" Homilies should be written down in Newman's judgment. Why? Here is his answer:

> I think that writing is a stimulus to the mental faculties, to the logical talent, to originality, to the power of illustration, to the arrangement of topics, second to none. Till a man begins to put down his thoughts about a subject on paper he will not ascertain what he knows and what he does not know; and still less will he be able to express what he does know.

Writing out the homily enables real clarity of thought to emerge, as one struggles with the ideas, reaches for clarity, striving for the spiritual good of the hearers and oneself. Newman offers another reason, and it is that writing out the homily may prevent a preacher from wandering all round the theological and spiritual world, moving like a free spirit through a free association of ideas, so that each homily becomes a virtual encyclopedia. Needless to say, Newman puts it more felicitously:

> Such a practice [as writing] will secure them against venturing upon really *ex tempore* matter. The more ardent a man is, and the greater power he has of affecting his hearers, so much the more will he need self-control and sustained recollection, and feel the advantage of committing himself, as it were, to the custody of his previous intentions, instead of yielding to any chance current of thought which rushes upon him in the midst of his preaching. His very gifts may need the counterpoise of more ordinary and homely accessories, such as the drudgery of composition.

Self-control, sustained reflection, avoiding the constant temptation of yielding to any chance thought that crosses one's mind, and, notice Newman's own phrase, "the drudgery of composition." Preaching is hard work, exciting work, but hard work. Composition in preaching flows only from the disciplined habits of prayer, study, and word crafting. Having committed his homily carefully, to writing, however, Newman does not think that it ought then to be read. For him **"a read sermon is a dead sermon."**

> While, then, a preacher will find it becoming and advisable to put into writing any important discourse beforehand, he will find it equally a point of propriety and expedience not to read it in the pulpit....If he employs a manuscript, the more he appears to dispense with it, the more he looks off from it, and directly addresses his audience, the more will he be considered to preach....Preaching is not reading, and reading is not preaching."[11]

Having outlined all that goes into homily preparation, it might be interesting to discover what Newman himself was like as a preacher.

Newman the Preacher

Newman was appointed vicar of St. Mary's in 1828, the church of the University of Oxford. The church was full when Newman preached, with, it is estimated, between five and six hundred undergraduates and graduates, as well as others.[12] The others would have included local shopkeepers, merchants, and numerous university servants. Newman preached from the pulpit of St. Mary's for the next sixteen years at the afternoon service at 4:00 p.m. on Sundays and feast days. The Victorians were interested in buying and reading volumes of sermons, and Newman's sold very well indeed, not least because they were recognized even then as "undoubted classics of Christian spirituality."[13]

What would it have been like to listen to Newman preach? Almost universally his hearers witnessed to the power of his preaching. One who heard him often, J. A. Froude, spoke of the psychological penetration of Newman's preaching: "He seemed to be addressing the most secret consciousness of each of us—as the eyes of a portrait appear to look at every person in a room."[14] That is no small accomplishment, the sense that the preacher is speaking directly to one. Another contemporary, the famous Matthew Arnold of Rugby, had this to say of Newman the preacher: "Who could resist the charm of that spiritual apparition, gliding in the dim afternoon light through the aisles of St. Mary's, rising into the pulpit, and then, in the most entrancing of voices, breaking the silence with words and thoughts which were a religious music—subtle, sweet, mournful."[15] Notice immediately this remark about musical composition that so frequently comes to mind when thinking of Newman as a preacher. Theologically, Matthew Arnold was at some considerable distance from Newman, so that this description is quite an accolade. The church of St. Mary would have been quite dark, creating something of a receptive atmosphere, accentuated by the gas lamp and the shadowy outline of the preacher. With little natural light, with very little to distract, the ambience of the church led to a great concentration on the preacher and what he had to say.

Not everyone who heard Newman preach, of course, was impressed and entranced like Froude and Arnold. For example, in 1838, a sectarian preacher from Philadelphia, John Alonzo Clark, enormously suspicious of Catholics and on the lookout for "the cloven hoof of Popery," but interested in contemporary approaches to preaching, was advised to go to Oxford to hear Newman preach. His reaction to a sermon at St. Mary's from the celebrated preacher was not quite the same as Froude or Arnold. He describes Newman as "[a] thin, sallow-looking man...cold in the pulpit as an icicle," and the sermon as "exceedingly dull and uninteresting."[16]

The present-day homilist Walter J. Burghardt, SJ, who has published volumes of his own homilies as well as a handbook on preaching, writes of Newman's skills in word crafting:

> In my early Jesuit days, it was not so much Newman's ideas that captivated me as his mastery of language. The words he chose always seemed so right; he could sustain, as few since, the periodic sentence; and the language was instinct with love. And so we young Jesuits imitated him, not to plagiarize *but to get his feel for words, for style, for the ordering of a clause, a sentence, a paragraph...how to use language with reverence, with care, with discrimination, with feeling.*[17]

This in no wise demands a use of words designed to impress. The Oratorian fathers who were Newman's colleagues in Birmingham noted that he spoke in the pulpit much as he spoke on ordinary occasions.[18] If there is a continuum of education, conversation, and formal preaching, one would expect there to be some continuum in the care with which words are used. Newman constantly exercised such care. The careful choice of words, the seeking after just the right expression in the pulpit echoed the no-less-careful choice of words in conversation, in letter writing, and indeed in his theological writing. It has been reckoned that the average length of Newman's sermons was fourteen pages, which took about forty-five minutes to deliver.[19]

Apparently, the practice was quite well established in England at the time—and experience of contemporary homiletic services by some of the ordained suggests that it has by no means disappeared—of reading the sermons prepared by someone else, perhaps published sermons, at the Sunday service. Newman almost never did this. In point of fact, he read three times sermons prepared by his close friend Hurrell Froude. One month after Froude's death in 1836, he tells us that he "read one of dear H.F.'s sermons(s) (on his birthday) being the first not my own I ever read in my life."[20] He read two others that year. This is Newman's grief preaching, not a model for imitation.[21]

There is an inescapable sense in which preaching is autobiographical. Our own experience, our own lives, our reading and education, the movies we see, the newspapers we read—all are necessary grist to the preaching mill. Overt autobiographical comment is another thing. Though it is impossible at times not to see connections between his preaching and the events of his own life, self-reference did not enter much into Newman's sermons. "What is truly startling and distinctive in his sermons is the absence of the pronoun 'I.' It appears in 'The Parting of Friends,'" for instance, only in biblical quotations and through the formulaic phrase 'my brethren'; in this sermon, delivered on the most piercing occasion in his life to that time, Newman appears as 'one' and 'he.'"[22] "One" and "he" rather than "I," the third person rather than the first person. Instead of dwelling on the events of his own life, Newman tends to interpret that life through scripture, the liturgy, and the doctrine of the church. He *inhabits* the language of scripture, liturgy, and doctrine so that he speaks out of this language.

"The Parting of Friends," his final sermon as a priest of the Church of England, delivered in the church of Littlemore on September 25, 1843, is particularly powerful. It would be almost another two years before he was received by the Italian Passionist, Dominic Barberi, into the Catholic Church, but there was a general sense that he was on his way. Many wept in the church, as they intuited Newman's farewell. His concluding words to his Anglican companions and friends are moving indeed:

> And O, my brethren, O kind and affectionate hearts,
> O loving friends, should you know anyone whose lot
> it has been, by writing or by word of mouth, in some
> degree to help you thus to act; if he has ever told you
> what you knew about yourselves, or what you did not
> know; has read to you your wants or feelings, and
> comforted you by the very reading: has made you feel

that there was a higher life than this daily one, and a brighter world than that you see; or encouraged you, or sobered you, or opened a way to the inquiring, or soothed the perplexed, if what he has said or done has ever made you take interest in him, and feel well inclined towards him; remember such a one in time to come, though you hear him not, and pray for him, that in all things he may know God's will, and at all times he may be ready to fulfil it.[23]

What beautiful and moving words, yet laconic in their autobiographical reference! At the end of this sermon, Newman took off his academic hood and threw it over the altar rails of the church, indicating, it seemed, that he had ceased to be a preacher and teacher in the Church of England.

Some Aspects of His Content

Like the great patristic liturgical preachers, Newman emphasized the holiness of the Christian life. "We dwell in the full light of the gospel, and the full grace of the Sacraments. We ought to have the holiness of Apostles. There is no reason except our own willful corruption, that we are not by this time walking in the steps of St. Paul or St. John, and following them as they followed Christ."[24] This is no abstract holiness that Newman commends. His sermons were and are practical and concrete, and very realistic.

> Nothing is more difficult than to be disciplined and regular in our religion. It is very easy to be religious by fits and starts, and to keep up our feelings by artificial stimulants; but regularity seems to trammel us, and we become impatient....Is not holiness the result of many patient, repeated efforts after obedience,

gradually working on us, and first modifying and then changing our hearts?[25]

The real problem, as Newman saw it, is self-deception, and so his purpose as a preacher is to lead his congregation "to some true notion of the depths and deceitfulness of the heart, which we do not really know."[26] Human beings, even the most religious, are so often inconsistent.

> If we look to some of the most eminent saints of Scripture, we shall find their recorded errors to have occurred in those parts of their duty in which each had most trial, and generally showed obedience most perfect. *Faithful* Abraham through want of faith denied his wife. Moses, the *meekest* of men, was excluded from the land of promise for a passionate word. The *wisdom* of Solomon was seduced to bow down to idols. Barnabas again, the *son of consolation,* had a sharp contention with St. Paul."[27] Ian Ker considers that the theme of consistency and inconsistency was almost an obsession for Newman, but might that so-called obsession be nothing more than a pastoral consequence of the studied observance of human fragility?[28]

One of his most engaging sermons is entitled "The Danger of Accomplishments." In this sermon Newman complains about reading novels, which is, in some degree, problematic. "*We* have nothing *to do;* we read, are affected, softened or roused, and that is all; we cool again,—nothing comes of it."[29] This certainly could be a problem, reading being understood as an essentially passive activity. But what if something does actually come of it? It may be that the reading of literature, of novels, introduces the reader into a very rich world of imaginative experience that invites some degree of personal transformation. We know that Newman liked to read Trollope and Eliot, astute interpreters of human nature. So it would seem that he would

71

approve of such novels and movies as enlarge our capacity for empathy with others and invite us to a deeper compassion for the vulnerabilities of the human condition.

Newman the Poet

It is not possible to move to Hopkins without saying a brief word about Newman's great poem "The Dream of Gerontius." Some would claim that it is Newman's greatest poem, "filled with the overarching vision of Newman's whole life: the relationship between God and the individual soul, the challenge to be sanctified."[30] The "Dream" was written in 1865, just one year after the *Apologia pro Vita Sua,* and the author had the attention of the reading public. The poem is about the dying of an elderly Christian, Gerontius:

> Jesu, Maria—I am near to death,
> And thou art calling me; I know it now—
> Not by the token of this faltering breath,
> This chill at heart, this dampness on my brow,—
> Jesu, have mercy! Mary, pray for me!—
> 'Tis this new feeling, never felt before,
> Be with me, Lord, in my extremity!
> That I am going, that I am no more.[31]

Those last four words, "That I am no more," hold one's attention. One commentator writes: "The sheer existential 'horror' at the prospect of dropping into 'nothingness' which Newman frankly portrays is very modern."[32] As he lay dying, he has received the last sacraments, and now is surrounded by his friends, who make their way through the prayers for the dying. From the Roman Ritual, the priest prays:

> Profiscere, anima Christiana, de hoc mundo!
> Go forth upon thy journey, Christian soul!
> Go from this world!

> Go, in the name of God the omnipotent Father who
>   created thee!
> Go, in the name of Jesus Christ, our Lord,
> Son of the living God who bled for thee!
> Go, in the name of the Holy Spirit, who
> Hath been poured out on thee![33]

At the end of this prayer, the soul of the dead Gerontius speaks:

> I went to sleep; and now I am refreshed.
> A strange refreshment: for I feel in me
> An inexpressive lightness, and a sense
> Of freedom, as I were at length myself,
> And ne'er had been before. How still it is!
> I hear no more the busy beat of time…[34]

Gerontius is now accompanied by his guardian angel to come before God in judgment. He has no sense of fear, a fear he had in life, but now he says to his guardian spirit:

> Dear Angel, say,
> Why have I now no fear at meeting Him?
> Now that the hour is come, my fear is fled;
> And at this balance of my destiny,
> Now close upon me, I can look forward
> With a serenest joy.[35]

The soul of Gerontius passes the band of demons, the "false spirits," and hears the five choirs of angels singing:

> Praise to the Holiest in the height,
> And in the depth be praise:
> In all his words most wonderful;
> Most sure in all his ways.

If one follows through at this point the entire anthem sung by the angels, God's "elder race," it is clear that its central content is the incarnation and the redemption, which divinize human beings, God's "younger race." The angels hymn the redemption of humankind and the gracious embrace by God of angels and humans. Gerontius parts from his guardian angel to come before God, and his angel describes the scene:

> The eager spirit has darted from my hold,
> And, with the intemperate energy of love,
> Flies to the dear feet of Emmanuel.

In the loving presence of God-with-us, the soul reaches judgment, that is to say, recognizes his unworthiness, his unloveliness, and so prays:

> Take me away, and in the lowest deep
> There let me be...
> There will I sing my absent Lord and Love:—
> Take me away,
> That sooner I may rise, and go above,
> And see Him in the truth of everlasting day.

This vision of God as his judge, but a judge whose best name is Love, makes Gerontius "feel" his sinfulness. It is an immediate feeling on coming into God's loving presence. It is learning that

> The flame of Everlasting Love
> Doth burn ere it transform.[36]

This burning that transforms is purgatory, the purging of unloveliness in the presence of Everlasting Love. "Purgatory," as Paul McPartlan rightly has it, "is the state of grace where the process of *Christification* can be perfected."[37] It is heaven's door, not hell's threshold.

The "Dream of Gerontius" has become popular and well known, especially in its musical setting by Sir Edward Elgar, who thought of it as the best piece of music he had composed. The poem was popular in its own right, however, touching the hearts of many in that Victorian age. Newman had heard of a farmer who, when taken ill, used the "Dream" as his meditation and prayer. He also knew of its use by General Gordon as he prepared to die at the taking of Khartoum in 1868. William Gladstone wrote to Newman, comparing the "Dream" to Dante's *Paradiso.* Even Charles Kingsley, to whose slanders Newman had made detailed reply in his *Apologia,* found himself deeply moved by the "Dream of Gerontius."[38] It is probably true to say, however, that relatively few read the "Dream" or listen to Elgar's musical rendition today, but many read the poetry, the superior poetry of Newman's young convert, Gerard Manley Hopkins.

Hopkins: The Poet-Preacher

It is generally acknowledged that Gerard Manley Hopkins, SJ, was not regarded as a successful preacher by his peers, but whatever the reasons, this was not due to any lack of love for word crafting. Hopkins cared passionately about words and, as a consummate theological poet, used words deliberately to invite encounter with God. His years at Oxford as an undergraduate (1863–1867) demonstrated his interest in the onomatopoetic theory of language and in the vision of the Oxford Movement, now focused on the leadership of Newman's friend Edward Bouverie Pusey, the Regius Professor of Hebrew, to whom Hopkins had started confessing by 1865.[39] During this period he also fell under the spell of the great Anglican priest-poet George Herbert. This is not the place to launch into an exacting account of the poetry or theology of Gerard Manley Hopkins. The intention is rather to juxtapose Hopkins's poetry with Newman's preaching in order to draw out their mutual love of words, their skill in word crafting, to move the hearer or reader further into relationship with the Mystery of God, and briefly to bring out something of the sacramental quality of Hopkins's poetry.

Both preachers and poets love words, as they attempt to find just the appropriate expression for their meaning. Hopkins put into poetry what Newman, for the most part, put into preaching. Hopkins wrote in 1882: "God's utterance of himself in himself is God the Word, outside himself is this world. This world then is word, expression, news of God."[40] No novelty here, but rather a reiteration of the theological insight beginning with the Prologue to St. John's Gospel (John 1:3), finding metaphysical expression in Origen of Alexandria and trinitarian analogy in Augustine of Hippo and Thomas Aquinas.

Aidan Nichols writes of Hopkins: "Hopkins, looking at nature with the penetrating eye of an artist, found in it evidence of the divine creativity. He brought to life a commonplace of patristic and medieval theology, namely that nature is a book in which we read of God."[41] Nature as a book in which we read of God enabled Hopkins to see the presence of God everywhere, even in unexpected places and to use his poetry as a sacramental means of making readers and hearers aware. He wrote to his friend Robert Bridges: "If you do not like it, it is because there is something you have not seen and I see."[42] In the context of this letter the "it" has to do with a musical work, but the "it" may just as well speak to Hopkins's permeative sense of the divine Mystery. He has seen "it" and wishes to draw others into that seeing.[43]

As a Jesuit, Hopkins had studied theology in the very beautiful location of St. Beuno's in Wales. Wales, with all its wild beauty, was the perfect place to confirm his sense of God's presence. Hopkins speaks of "the Holy Ghost sent to us through creatures," "shewn *in operibus,*" so that "[a]ll things therefore are charged with love, are charged with God and if we know how to touch them give off sparks and take fire, yield drops and flow, ring and tell of him."[44] All of this becomes the context for his magnificent 1877 sonnet "God's Grandeur." It should also be noted that the year 1877 saw his ordination to the priesthood, an occasion of immense joy.

> The world is charged with the grandeur of God.
> It will flame out, like shining from shook foil.

This is not some escapist, romantic view of nature. Hopkins, as a Jesuit, had also served in the British industrial towns of

London, Liverpool, and Glasgow. He wrote to his old high school teacher Canon Dixon: "My Liverpool and Glasgow experiences laid upon my mind a conviction, a truly crushing conviction, of the misery of town life to the poor, and…of the misery of the poor in general, of the degradation even of our race, of the hollowness of the century's civilization."[45] He knew how greed and sin can disfigure God's creative presence:

> And all is seared with trade; bleared, smeared with
>   toil;
> And wears man's smudge and shares man's smell.

Nonetheless, God's indwelling of his creation cannot be eliminated by our human disfigurement. There is an asymmetrical relationship between God's grace and human sinfulness. God's grace is so much greater, and always ahead, so that Hopkins can write:

> And, for all this, nature is never spent;
>   There lives the dearest freshness deep down
>   things…
> Because the Holy Ghost over the bent
>   World broods with warm breast and with ah! bright
>   wings.

In his journal we find these words: "I thought how sadly beauty of inscape was unknown and buried away from simple people and yet how near at hand it was if they had eyes to see it and it could be called out everywhere again."[46] Beauty is sacramental, is close to ordinary people, but they need sacramental vision and a sacramental guide. Hopkins offered the vision and became the guide through his poems. This poetic offer of vision is, however, only possible because it is Hopkins's own vision. It is thoroughly his. Thus, it is a truism to affirm that "[t]he evidence of his love affair with God is unmistakably audible throughout his poetry."[47]

It may be claimed that Hopkins's religious poetry differs from other English religious poetry in the fact that he deliberately intends to be "pastoral."[48] What is meant by this is that he understood himself, behind the many things he did, as a working pastoral priest. A priest is a mystagogue, inviting and encouraging others into the mystery of God through any and every kind of sacramental conduit, and especially the sacrament of the church. Hopkins's poetry is a sacramental conduit, and deliberately so.

In another poem, "As Kingfishers Catch Fire," Hopkins outlines how each individual thing in God's good creation does its own thing:

> As kingfishers catch fire, dragonflies dráw fláme…
> Stones ring…
> Each mortal thing does one thing and the same…

Simultaneously, even as each thing does its own thing, as it were, God indwells the panorama of creation, is really present, albeit anonymously, for so many people:

> Í say móre: the just man justices;
> Kéeps gráce: thát keeps all his goings graces;
> Acts in God's eye what in God's eye he is—
> Chríst. For Christ plays in ten thousand places,
> Lovely in limbs, and lovely in eyes not his
> To the Father through the features of men's faces.

Behind, beneath, and above all creation is the indwelling God, especially in human beings, and most especially in the church. So, Hopkins says more. The more he says is that behind and beneath the just man is God, is Christ.

> …Christ plays in ten thousand places,
> Lovely in limbs, lovely in eyes not his
> To the Father through the features of men's faces.

These lines are, quite simply, a startling expression of God's intimate presence to and with us: Christ plays everywhere before the Father through us. Hans Urs von Balthasar comments on these three last lines of Hopkins: "Finally it is Christ himself, who is enselved in all his members if the believer will let grace work in himself and together with it breathe forth a sweet perfume to God...."[49] Hopkins would have approved mightily of the English translator of Balthasar's "enselved" here. It is a most Hopkinsian verb.

Hopkins finds God-in-Christ everywhere and expresses this finding, in a sacramental way, in poetry. The word crafting of the poem sacramentalizes the divine presence that is to be found everywhere and always. One contemporary student of Hopkins puts it like this: "The poet incarnates in poetry the Incarnate Christ, the enfleshed Logos who is the foundation of world and word....He saw the poet's task as crafting poetic language in such a way that it, like the sacraments, both signified the presence of Christ and encouraged the acknowledgment and reception of this presence by the hearer."[50] This is a very high theology of poetry indeed, a theology of poetry as sacramental preaching.

Conclusion

When it comes to the word crafting of preaching, there is rightly a widespread diversity of practice, but probably all who preach would agree that careful attention to preachers of the past pays dividends. Newman offers a pedagogy for homiletic proclamation, while Hopkins offers a mystagogy for poetic proclamation. The preacher-poet Newman, and the poet-preacher Hopkins may be nineteenth-century men, but their witness rings out across all ages.

Bibliography

Ballinger, Philip A. *The Poem as Sacrament: The Theological Aesthetic of Gerard Manley Hopkins.* Louvain: Peeters; Grand Rapids: Eerdmans, 2000.

Ker, Ian. *The Achievement of John Henry Newman.* Notre Dame, IN: University of Notre Dame Press, 1990.

Murray, Placid, OSB. *Newman the Oratorian.* Dublin: Gill and Macmillan, 1969.

Notes

1. Adapted from Ian Ker, *The Achievement of John Henry Newman* (Notre Dame, IN: University of Notre Dame Press, 1990), 95.
2. Philip A. Ballinger, *The Poem as Sacrament: The Theological Aesthetic of Gerard Manley Hopkins* (Louvain: Peeters; Grand Rapids: Eerdmans, 2000), 236.
3. Sheridan Gilley, "Newman and the Convert Mind," in *Newman and Conversion,* ed. Ian Ker (Notre Dame, IN: University of Notre Dame Press, 1997), 8.
4. Claude Colleer Abbott, ed., *The Letters of Gerard Manley Hopkins to Robert Bridges* (London: Oxford University Press, 1935), 5.
5. George W. Rutler, "Newman, John Henry," in *Concise Encyclopedia of Preaching,* ed. William H. Willimon and Richard Lischer (Louisville: Westminster John Knox Press, 1995), 345.
6. Ker, *Achievement of John Henry Newman,* 74.
7. Placid Murray, *Newman the Oratorian* (Dublin: Gill and Macmillan, 1969), 31.
8. Cited from Murray, *Newman the Oratorian,* 37.
9. John Henry Newman, *The Idea of a University* (London: Longmans Green, 1899), 406, 408, 411–12, 413.
10. Ibid., 415, 419.
11. Ibid., 421, 422–23, 424.
12. R. D. Middleton, "The Vicar of St. Mary's," in *John Henry Newman: Centenary Essays* (London: Burns, Oates and Washbourne, 1945), 131.
13. Ker, *Achievement of John Henry Newman,* 75.

14. J. A. Froude, *Short Studies on Great Subjects,* 4th series (New York: Charles Scribner's Sons, 1910), 186.

15. Cited in Middleton, "Vicar of St. Mary's," 131.

16. Cited in David J. DeLaura, "'O Unforgotten Voice': The Memory of Newman in the Nineteenth Century," *Renascence* 43 (1991): 82.

17. Walter J. Burghardt, SJ, *Preaching: The Art and the Craft* (Mahwah, NJ: Paulist Press, 1987), 193.

18. Eric Griffiths, "Newman: The Foolishness of Preaching," in *Newman after a Hundred Years,* ed. Ian Ker and Alan G. Hill (Oxford: Clarendon Press, 1990), 66.

19. Murray, *Newman the Oratorian,* 31.

20. *Letters and Diaries of John Henry Newman* (Oxford: Clarendon Press, 1988), 5:267.

21. See Griffiths, "Newman: The Foolishness of Preaching," 65 n. 11.

22. Ibid., 67.

23. *Sermons on Subjects of the Day,* New impression (London: Longmans Green, 1910), 409.

24. *Parochial and Plain Sermons* (London: Longmans Green, 1891), 1:13, 82.

25. Ibid., 1:11, 252.

26. Ibid., 1:27–28, 35, 172.

27. Ibid., 1:46–47.

28. Ker, *Achievement of John Henry Newman,* 89.

29. *Parochial and Plain Sermons,* 2:371.

30. Paul McPartlan, "Go Forth, Christian Soul," *One in Christ* 34 (1998): 248.

31. John Henry Newman, *The Dream of Gerontius* (Oxford: Mowbray, 1986), 1.

32. McPartlan, "Go Forth, Christian Soul," 251.

33. Newman, *Dream of Gerontius,* 9.

34. Ibid., 10–11.

35. Ibid., 21-22.

36. Ibid., 34.

37. McPartlan, "Go Forth, Christian Soul," 256.

38. Gregory Winterton, "Foreword," in Newman, *Dream of Gerontius,* viii–x.

39. For a fine discussion of the complexities of relationship between Pusey and Hopkins, see Alison G. Sulloway, *Gerard Manley Hopkins and the Victorian Temper* (London: Routledge and Kegan Paul, 1972), 56–63.

40. Christopher Devlin, SJ, ed., *Sermons and Devotional Writings of Gerard Manley Hopkins* (London: Oxford University Press, 1959), 129.

41. Aidan Nichols, OP, *The Shape of Catholic Theology* (Collegeville, MN: Liturgical Press, 1991), 19.

42. Abbott, *Letters of Gerard Manley Hopkins to Robert Bridges,* 214.

43. See Virginia R. Ellis, *Gerard Manley Hopkins and the Language of Mystery* (Columbia, MO/London: University of Missouri Press, 1991), passim, but especially in summary form, pp. 4–8.

44. Devlin, *Sermons and Devotional Writings of Gerard Manley Hopkins,* 195; see also the discussion, albeit more literary, in Ellis, *Gerard Manley Hopkins and the Language of Mystery,* 124–33.

45. Claude Colleer Abbott, ed. *The Correspondence of Gerard Manley Hopkins and Richard Watson Dixon,* 2nd ed. (London: Oxford University Press, 1955), 97.

46. Cited in W. H. Gardner, ed., *Gerard Manley Hopkins: Poems and Prose* (Harmondsworth: Penguin Books, 1985), xxi.

47. Sulloway, *Gerard Manley Hopkins and the Victorian Temper,* 5.

48. See Ian Ker, *The Catholic Revival in English Literature 1845–1961* (Notre Dame, IN: University of Notre Dame Press, 2003), 50.

49. Hans Urs von Balthasar, *The Glory of the Lord: A Theological Aesthetics, vol. 3, Studies in Theological Style: Lay Styles* (San Francisco: Ignatius Press, 1986), 384–85.

50. Ballinger, *Poem as Sacrament,* 228–30.

5
ISAAC THOMAS HECKER (1819–1888)

Hecker was instinctively Catholic, not exclusive. His ability to see the partial truth on both sides of a dispute and the justice in each of two conflicting claims is most impressive when he approaches problems that involve the relationship of nature and grace, of freedom and authority, of the outer and inner elements of religion.

—Joseph McSorley[1]

Only Newman of his English-speaking contemporaries was more misunderstood.

—David J. O'Brien[2]

Historian David O'Brien opens his biography of Isaac Hecker with these words:

Isaac Thomas Hecker loved to tell his story. Perhaps no American of the nineteenth century was as convinced that his own life embodied the meaning of the national experience....He wanted to build a "Catholic America," which would lead the way to a "Catholic World." In pursuit of that dream, he became famous as a preacher, lecturer, writer-editor, founder of an important religious community and, after his death, center of a major international theological dispute."[3]

The international theological dispute had to do with "Americanism," during the pontificate of Leo XIII and is best left to that chapter. Here we shall concentrate on Hecker's life, weaving into that life something of the church's story, both nationally and internationally.

Becoming a Catholic

Isaac Thomas Hecker was born on December 18, 1819, in New York, the youngest child of German immigrants John Hecker, a metalworker, and Susan Caroline Friend. The family was poor, but prepared through sheer hard work to improve their socioeconomic situation. One son, Henry, died in infancy. Isaac's siblings were John (b. 1812), Elizabeth (b. 1816), and George (b. 1818). John Hecker had his own brass foundry, but it closed first around 1824, and then finally in 1828. Although he lived until 1860, Isaac's father disappeared from the family's life, and his mother, Susan, a devout Methodist, became the dominant influence in her young family. There can be little doubt that Susan's Methodism was to shape and mold her children. We hear mention in letters of John Hecker Senior's "problem," but no information as to what that "problem" was. The two older brothers, John and George, opened what was eventually to become a very successful baking business in order to provide support for the family. In terms of religious development, John was to become an Episcopalian and George was to follow his brother Isaac into the Catholic Church—but this is to race ahead. Isaac attended a public school until he was thirteen, when he left to work and make his contribution to the family, initially as a messenger for the Methodist Book Concern, and then for his brothers.

The Hecker brothers were involved in local politics, and, in the context of this involvement, Isaac heard a lecture in March 1841 by the well-known Boston editor and reformer Orestes Brownson. Brownson made quite an impression on the young man, and when he returned to lecture in New York in January 1842, he was invited to stay with the Heckers and so had conversations with Isaac. Brownson's perspective gave emphasis to human progress and to the felt need for a more democratic Christianity in tune with the times.

In the spring or early summer of 1842, Isaac Hecker had what can only be called a conversion experience, described by David O'Brien in these terms: "The experience constituted perhaps the central moment of Isaac Hecker's life."[4] The experience provided him with "in a sense a new creation, a development of a deeper life, a new dispensation unfolding a new law of his being," words he recorded in his journal the following year.[5] It was a turning point in his life, marked by the determination to remain celibate. At least on the surface, there is a certain parallelism to Newman's conversion experience and subsequent decision for celibacy.

The end of 1842 found Isaac visiting the Brownsons near Boston, having quite suddenly departed from the family home in New York. He was restless, however, and soon attached himself, at Brownson's suggestion, to Brook Farm, near Boston, a utopian community much inspired by transcendentalism and constituted by what we might today call well-established social dropouts. In time Hecker was to meet the major transcendentalists Ralph Waldo Emerson and Henry David Thoreau. The transcendentalism of New England and of Brook Farm was a reform movement in which the essence of religion was to be found within the person, in the inner realm of spirit, not in doctrine and dogma. The inner spirit and its freedom were what counted, not external structures imposed by conventional society. The work of Brook Farm centered on teaching in the community school, but it also involved the ordinary range of chores and responsibilities necessary for the support and upkeep of the community. Here the largely unschooled and uneducated Hecker baked for the community and spent his time in the study of Christianity, especially in its French and German Romantic expression. His study also took him to the point where the spirit within was interpreted as the Holy Spirit, the Holy Spirit indwelling and leading the church, and so to the need for ritual, doctrine, and structure. Initially, he was led to the Episcopal Church, and in the first quarter of 1843 he was reading the Oxford Movement's *Tracts for the Times,* and most notably the tracts authored by John Henry Newman.

Isaac's friend Orestes Brownson was seriously considering Catholicism, and undoubtedly that had some influence upon him. After all, Hecker revered Brownson. Nevertheless, it was Hecker's own independent journey, his own inner experience of spirit/Spirit that brought him to Catholicism. In April of 1843 Hecker first encountered the Roman Catholic Church during the Easter services. The experience, supported by his reading and study, had such an impact on him that he wrote: "The Catholic Church alone seems to satisfy my wants my faith life soul....I may be laboring under a delusion....Yet my soul is Catholic and that faith answers responds to my soul in its religious aspirations and its longings I have not wished to make myself Catholic but it answers to the wants of my soul it answers on all sides."[6] Nonetheless, his studies continued with a reading of Johann Adam Möhler and Immanuel Kant and a study of the Anglican claims. He was going through a spiritual turmoil that took him in discussion to others as he quested resolution and tranquility. Finally, Hecker was baptized a Catholic by Bishop John McCloskey in New York on August 1, 1844, over a year before Newman's reception into the church. O'Brien comments: "The reason for his conversion was primarily personal. It was a decision to submit fully and finally to the Holy Spirit within....The spirit in the church and the spirit who spoke from within were the same spirit."[7]

From the Redemptorists to the Paulists

It was inevitable that a man of Hecker's disposition, a seeker after the Spirit, would consider the priesthood. In this he was encouraged by Bishop John Hughes of New York, as well as by his coadjutor, Bishop McCloskey, who had baptized Hecker. On April 24, 1845, he came into contact with Gabriel Rumpler, a Redemptorist priest working in his congregation's New York parish. Along with two former seminarians of the Episcopal General Theological Seminary in New York, James McMaster and Clarence Walworth, Hecker turned to Rome as a result of the Oxford Movement and found himself bound for Europe, to the Redemptorist novitiate at St. Trond, Belgium. The group arrived in London in late August. McMaster went to visit his hero, John Henry Newman, at Littlemore in Oxford, but unaccompanied by Walworth or Hecker, who were anxious to make headway and arrive at St. Trond. "Hecker found in the Redemptorist Rule and exercises, and in Catholic spiritual writers, a conceptual structure to make sense of his own experience."[8]

After the novitiate, Hecker went on to the Redemptorist house of studies, where he encountered difficulties that arose in part probably from his lack of experience with formal classes and disciplined study. He persevered with the Redemptorists, however, and they with him, and he was ordained a priest by Cardinal Nicholas Wiseman of Westminster on October 23, 1849. As part of the Redemptorist community at Clapham, he did mission work in and around London and met the converts from Anglicanism, Henry Edward Manning, later to be archbishop of Westminster, and Frederick Faber, later to be the founder of the Brompton Oratory. Eventually in early 1851 he sailed for New York. Isaac Hecker had been away from America for almost six years. He was ready to return.

With his brother priests, he threw himself into in the mission work that was characteristic of the Redemptorists. A parish mission was designed to renew the vitality of the parish through vigorous preaching on the eternal verities, on sacramental confession and communion, and on the renewal of baptismal vows at the end of the mission. David O'Brien reports that this English-language band of missionaries gave the first organized mission in English in the United States in New York. It was very successful, and soon they had more mission work than they could handle. Tensions were to develop on three fronts. The first had to do with missionary work. Parish missions of their nature are directed to Catholics, but Hecker had this passionate desire to evangelize among non-Catholics. "We must make Yankeedom," he wrote, "the Rome of the modern world, or at least work hard to make it Catholic."[9] To further this project and with the support of his superiors, in 1855 Hecker wrote a book entitled *Questions of the Soul.*

> The book was an almost perfect expression of American self-culture....The freedom to choose, to define for oneself the terms of life, was the fundamental context for Hecker's argument....He raised fundamental questions about human nature and history, all arising from that sense of the American, beginning anew, free from the prejudice of the past, prepared to follow reason and trust intuition.[10]

The book was very successful, especially with non-Catholics, and received warm praise from Orestes Brownson. It is best described as "a romantic apologetic of the restless heart," aimed at the New England seekers whom he knew so well and among whom he had sought and sojourned.[11] The second area of tension arose between the American and German Redemptorists. In 1849, after Hecker and his companions had gone to Europe for formation, the Redemptorists established a novitiate in Baltimore. The Germans tended to emphasize an unquestioned submission to authority, something that did not sit well with native-born Americans, and the Germans also tended to find fault with the American predilection for missionary work over the care of parishes. Third, culturally the Americans were more optimistic about human nature than their German counterparts, trained in Europe and heirs to centuries of European custom, tradition, and thought patterns. Americans, on the other hand, took democracy as axiomatic, with all its freedoms and novelties.

Another book by Hecker reached the public in 1857, *Aspirations of Nature.* It was not as well received as his first book, not least because his thesis embroiled him in fundamental questions of the relationship between reason and faith—indeed, issues that would be tackled at the First Vatican Council in 1870. The book was aimed at those "whose disenchantment with Calvinist orthodoxy took the form of William Ellery Channing's Unitarianism."[12] The new book was intended to show that the doctrines and practices of Catholicism were eminently reasonable and almost "naturally" designed to meet the needs of genuine seekers after God. It was a very American project, an optimistic project. The emphasis was less on human sinfulness, on original sin—though it is important to recognize that Hecker never denied this reality. Rather, he wished to emphasize that, despite human sinfulness, there was an innate, verifiable aspiration in human nature for God, and this innate aspiration could be shown to find its most perfect and satisfactory expression in Catholicism. It was a way of doing theology, of setting out an apologetic for the church that was very different and much more hopeful than the dominant approach. William Portier rightly describes Hecker as an "American Catholic empirical theologian," "a typically American religious thinker."[13] Yet it could be shown that Hecker's vision recalls that of Irenaeus, bishop of Lyons in the second century, who espoused a more optimistic anthropology than that of his later Latin counterpart Augustine of Hippo. Augustine, for a complex variety of reasons—not least his own experience—held to a rather pessimistic view of human nature as a result of the fall of Adam and Eve. Irenaeus believed in the fall, yes, but saw it as more of an adolescent experimental mistake, and so he was more hopeful of humankind's recapitulation in Christ. Isaac Hecker was more Irenaean than Augustinian.

The developing tensions now came to a head. The American born, English-speaking Redemptorists, with Hecker as their "leader," had reached the conclusion that it was necessary to establish a separate house for the English-speaking mission band, preferably in New York. They were concerned that care of parishes, and the rumored increasing demand of parishes, would seriously undermine their mission work. They approached Archbishop Hughes of New York, who was supportive, as was also Isaac's brother George, who pledged financial assistance for such a house. Needless to relate, the Redemptorist provincial superior, Fr. Ruland, was incensed at this development, about which he had not been informed. It was suggested by the Americans that Hecker, armed with a raft of episcopal testimonials, go to Rome to make the case before the superior general, Fr. Nicholas Mauron, and Cardinal Alexander Barnabo, head of the Propaganda, the Vatican office that dealt with American church questions. The entire scheme was open to a host of misinterpretations. Was this an anti-German position, leading to schism in the Redemptorist congregation? Did this show a lack of due deference to authority, especially since it had been forbidden by their Roman superior for Redemptorists to go to Rome? In the midst of this maelstrom of misinterpretation, aided and abetted by correspondence between America and Rome, Hecker sailed on August 5, 1857.

Hecker wrote a letter to his brother George from London, where he shared his views with friends from his Clapham days, including Manning and Faber. The letter conveys not only something of Hecker's immediate sentiments but also something of his ongoing vision for America and American Catholicism.

Strange to say I find no men animated with a view of a better future. I did my best to excite it, but somehow or other men's heads in Europe are turned quite around. They see the past but cannot fix their gaze on the future. But they all admit that for us in the U.S. there is a prospect of something better....The Church now stands pretty much in status quo. No one is actuated by hope and the energies which ought to be directed to her interests are wasted in great measure in private bickerings.[14]

The letter is dated August 24 and anticipates the difficult times and trials Hecker was to experience in Rome.

It was the Rome of the increasingly beleaguered Pio Nono, whose affair with liberalism was decidedly over, and it was the Rome of growing ultramontanism. When Isaac arrived in Rome on August 26, his fate had already been decided. The Redemptorist superior general, Fr. Mauron, advised him that his very trip, contrary to Redemptorist policy, was already grounds for dismissal from the congregation, and so he was dismissed without a hearing. Cardinal Barnabo at Propaganda, on the other hand, was far more receptive, albeit with curial caution. Hecker communicated to his colleagues back in the States that the best way forward seemed to be starting out on their own, free of the Redemptorists, through the creation of a religious congregation more adapted to the actual needs of evangelization in modern America. His American colleagues were initially far from unanimous in support of his proposal, but in fact that is what transpired. "Hecker had no doubts about their status; they were free to form a new community under the authority of a bishop of their own choosing. When Walworth notified their supporters of the Roman decision, he told them that separation from the Redemptorists had taken place 'charitably and kindly,' and the pope had given them 'encouragement to go on and form a new society.'"[15] This was to be the Paulists.

Vatican I and After

The new religious society met in New York when Hecker returned in May 1858, with the encouragement of Archbishop Hughes that they make his city and diocese their permanent home. They formed a provisional rule, not unlike that of St. Philip Neri's Oratorians, which was approved by Hughes on July 7, as the Congregation of the Missionary Priests of St. Paul the Apostle. Archbishop Hughes gave them the care of a parish in New York with their superior, Isaac Hecker, as the *ex officio* pastor. Hughes's insistence on their having care of a parish stemmed from the shortage of priests to serve his growing diocese. Requests for parish missions continued to grow. Hughes's support of the fledgling community was real, even as he found Hecker's vision uncomfortable. The archbishop was very suspicious of projects that attempted to establish consonance between Catholicism and the American Constitution. By April 1859 the Paulists had the needed endorsement of the Roman Congregation of Bishops and Regulars. The community began to grow, but slowly.

In October of 1859 they found a new recruit in Robert Tillotson, an American and a member of Newman's Oratory in Birmingham. He joined with Newman's blessing. Clarence Walworth, who for various reasons had felt unable to stay with the new community in 1858, returned in 1861, but was to leave again some years later. The Paulists needed new members because of their double responsibility, the maintenance of their parish and the preaching of missions. They worked hard at both. In point of fact, the parish, St. Paul's, quickly became a center of homiletic and liturgical excellence. David O'Brien describes the preaching: "While American Catholic piety at the time was increasingly negative, emphasizing human depravity and the temptations of the world, the Paulist sermons were characteristically positive, aiming at the sanctification of the souls of parishioners in the midst of everyday life."[16] They paid special attention to liturgical music and singing. In many respects, St. Paul's became a model of ecclesial renewal after the manner of Vatican II, but before Vatican I!

Paulist activity, under the Heckers' direction—Isaac's energy and vision and George's money—entered the world of publishing in 1865 with a magazine entitled *Catholic World,* carrying articles on theology, philosophy, church issues, and literature. Among the many and varied items *Catholic World* published was John Henry Newman's "Dream of Gerontius." The connection with Newman goes further. The aim of the journal was to inform not only the clergy but also the laity, and in that sense it was coincident with Newman's vision of an informed and educated laity, conscious of their identity as church.

To aid in the religious education and formation of poorer people, Hecker now suggested the publication of short and inexpensive tracts or pamphlets and the establishment of the Catholic Publication Society. This was attractive to Archbishop Martin John Spalding of Baltimore, who not only supported the venture but also arranged for Hecker to bring it to the attention of the bishops assembled for the Second Plenary Council of Baltimore in 1866. Hecker spoke to the bishops as follows in a sermon entitled "The Church's Future Triumph": "Nowhere is there a promise of a brighter future for the Church than in our own country. Here, thanks to our American Constitution, the Church is free to do her divine work. Here she finds a civilization in harmony with her divine teachings. Here, Christianity is promised a reception from an intelligent and free people, that will bring forth a development of unprecedented glory." It was a unique opportunity for Hecker to lay out his classic vision for America before all the bishops. As O'Brien remarks, "At the Baltimore Council in 1866 Isaac Hecker was at the peak of his career."[17]

The following year, 1867, Hecker attended another important assembly, the Catholic Congress in Malines, Belgium. Along with one of his priest-brothers, Fr. Hewit, he sought writers and subscriptions for *Catholic World* and the Catholic Publication Society. The priests visited both Manning and

Newman, among others, and the latter wrote to his friend Ambrose St. John that Hecker was "fluent, clever, just the man to propagate Catholic truth among the Yankees."[18] At the congress, Hecker delivered an address entitled "Report on the Present Religious Condition of the United States." He could not have been unaware of the ongoing tensions in Malines between the ultramontanists and the more progressive wing of the church, but he was not particularly interested. His concern was the church in America, and just possibly a parallel American Catholic Congress.

Pope Pius IX summoned the bishops of the world to a council in the Vatican in 1869. Though neither a bishop nor a major religious superior, Hecker was invited by Bishop Sylvester Rosecrans of Columbus, Ohio, who was unwell, to serve as his procurator, but later Hecker became *peritus* theologian to the up-and-coming Bishop James Gibbons of North Carolina. Orestes Brownson wrote of this appointment to his son Henry: "Father Hecker goes to the Council as procurator for Bishop Rosecrans. He is growing less radical and will no doubt return from Rome as conservative as I."[19] Brownson did not get it quite right! En route to the council on the same ship were Archbishop Thomas Connolly of Halifax, Nova Scotia, and Archbishop Peter Kenrick of St. Louis, both bishops opposed to the ultramontanist claim of papal infallibility. Hecker also visited Newman in England, and he was clearly not in favor of the definition of papal infallibility. He was technically what came to be known as an "inopportunist." Hecker was thus allied with the anti-infallibilists, particularly with their representatives in the American hierarchy. It seems that his opposition to infallibility had to do in the main with the collegiality and the independence of the bishops, which he judged to be severely undermined by the ultramontane views. At the same time, and without Hecker's support, Fr. Hewit had published in *Catholic World* a strong pro-infallibilist article. This made for tensions between the two men. Ultimately, of course, the pro-infallibilists had the upper hand when it came to the council vote, but they did not achieve the comprehensive definition for which many of them, especially Archbishop Manning, had hoped. If the likes of Archbishop Manning were disappointed with the restricted scope of the conciliar definition, for Hecker and those who thought like him "the definition appeared to conflict with the democratic temper of the age."[20] Nevertheless, he accepted the definition. Hecker returned home from Vatican I disappointed but determined to pour his energies into the Paulists and their work for evangelization.

The Final Years

There had always been differences between Isaac Hecker and Orestes Brownson, but the difference became very sharp in the wake of Vatican I. Hecker was more open to the American democratic experiment, Brownson less so. Brownson wrote to Hecker in 1870: "Catholicity is theologically compatible with democracy, as you and I would explain democracy, but practically there is, in my judgement, no compatibility between them."[21] Brownson saw democracy as coming from below, whereas real power comes from above, from God. He saw Hecker conforming the church to the age and to the culture, but he believed that true evangelization consisted in the conformity of the culture to the church. These differences in ecclesiology may be taken a stage further. Brownson saw the church primarily as the body of Christ and gave emphasis to its visibility and its structures. Hecker, on the other hand, gave primacy to the church as the dwelling place of the Spirit, which led him to stress the inner "spiritual" nature of the church.[22] Arguably, Hecker's ecclesiology was always pneumatological. From his earliest religious stirrings after his conversion experience, he had experienced the spirit, the inner call and direction, and then identified this with the Holy Spirit in a formal ecclesiology. Though the two men continued to respect each other, it was impossible for them to see eye to eye. The lens through which they viewed both modernity and the church was too different. Yet, when Brownson died in

1876, Hecker wrote to the family: "I owe much, and more, perhaps to your father than to any other man in my early life. My friendship and sense of gratitude to him has never been affected by any event during forty years. No man has done more disinterestedly what he considered to be his duty."[23]

Hecker's own health was far from robust, most probably a combination of both psychological challenges and the normal physical deterioration in life, though John Farina, a Hecker specialist, believes Isaac suffered from chronic leukemia. In summer 1873 he set off on a prolonged vacation, which, it was hoped, would restore his good health. His itinerary took him throughout Europe but also to Egypt, with a trip up the Nile. In November 1874, he set out his ideas concerning the church in a manuscript with the title, *An Exposition of the Church in View of Recent Difficulties and Controversies and the Present Needs of the Church.* In this text he universalizes his vision of the Catholic Church in America. This is how John Farina describes Hecker's vision of the church: "From his earliest days Hecker had envisioned God in terms of universal Spirit—a life-giving, effective force that was the very action of God, creating and sustaining all things....'The Holy Spirit is at work among Chinese, Moslems, and all nations, and tribes, in every rational soul.'"[24] Hecker now wants to be nothing less than a universal Catholic, recognizing and encouraging and building on God's Spirit wherever it is to be found.

Copies of the book were sent to Manning and Newman. Manning found himself in general agreement with Hecker's book in a letter to the author of February 1, 1875: "In the general outline I heartily agree. And I especially hold that the low state of mind in respect to the Office of the Holy Ghost in the Church has caused most of our modern errors; and forgetfulness of His presence in us has made us unspiritual and merely natural." Newman, Manning's *bête noire,* said that the book was "clear, interesting and winning," but he was far from Hecker's optimism. He wrote to Hecker on April 10: "Whereas you infer 'we are so bad we are sure to get better,' I feel there is another inference conceivable and possible in fact: 'we are so bad off, that we are likely to get worse.'"[25] Newman, perhaps with a more detailed and informed reading of history on his side, responded to Hecker with a theological version of Murphy's Law: If things can get worse, they will get worse! Back home, by mid-summer 1875, the Paulists were increasingly frustrated with Hecker. They needed him, his guidance, and his counsel. They wanted him home. He returned in October 1875.

Though still unwell, he continued to work and to write. In 1886 he pulled his more recent publications together in a book entitled *The Church and the Age,* in which was found "the strongest affirmation of democracy and human rights yet written by a Catholic American."[26] The key to Hecker's vision of the church, as really it had always been, was the Holy Spirit acting in people's lives. He is fully supportive in the book of the church's authority and structures, but at the same time he reaffirms that cardinal theological principle of his youth: "The exclusive view of the external authority of the Church, without a proper understanding of the nature and work of the Holy Spirit in the soul, would render the practice of religion formal, obedience servile, and the Church sterile."[27]

Conclusion

Isaac Hecker died on December 22, 1888. To Fr. Hewit, Newman wrote of Hecker some weeks later in February of 1889 that he thought there was "a sort of unity in our lives," that they had both "begun a work of the same kind."[28] Both Hecker and Newman were concerned with conversion, but from very different perspectives. Newman, having come through the Oxford Movement in the Church of England, came to Catholicism through study and thought. Hecker, having come through the transcendentalism of New England, also came to Catholicism through study and thought. But, whereas Newman probably found his work for conversion expressed primarily in and through the witness of his writings, Hecker found his work expressed in the natural attraction of Catholicism allied to the natural optimism of Americans. Neither found himself integrally accepted by the very people whom he desired to serve.

Bibliography

Farina, John. *An American Experience of God: The Spirituality of Isaac Hecker.* Ramsey, NJ: Paulist Press, 1981.

O'Brien, David J. *Isaac Hecker, An American Catholic.* Mahwah, NJ: Paulist Press, 1992.

Notes

1. Joseph McSorley, *Father Hecker and His Friends* (St. Louis: B. Herder, 1953), 171.

2. David J. O'Brien, "Isaac Hecker, Catholicism and Modern Society," in *Hecker Studies: Essays on the Thought of Isaac Hecker,* ed. John Farina (Ramsey, NJ: Paulist Press, 1983), 126.

3. David J. O'Brien, *Isaac Hecker, An American Catholic* (Mahwah, NJ: Paulist Press, 1992), 7. I am heavily reliant on this magisterial study of Hecker.

4. Ibid., 19.

5. Ibid., 20.

6. Diary entry for April 24, cited in O'Brien, *Isaac Hecker,* 33.

7. O'Brien, *Isaac Hecker,* 65.

8. Ibid., 88.

9. In a letter cited in O'Brien, *Isaac Hecker,* 104.

10. O'Brien, *Isaac Hecker,* 105.

11. William L. Portier, *Isaac Hecker and the First Vatican Council* (Lewiston, NY: Edward Mellen Press, 1985), 2; see also the similar description of Patrick Carey, *The Roman Catholics* (Westport, CT: Greenwood Press, 1983), 41–42.

12. Portier, *Isaac Hecker and the First Vatican Council,* 3.

13. In his dissertation, "Providential Nation: An Historical-Theological Study of Isaac Hecker's 'Americanism'" (Ph.D. diss., University of Toronto, 1990), cited in O'Brien, *Isaac Hecker,* 125.

14. O'Brien, *Isaac Hecker,* 121.

15. Ibid., 166.

16. Ibid., 187.

17. Ibid., 206.

18. Cited in O'Brien, *Isaac Hecker,* 215.

19. Cited in Portier, *Isaac Hecker and the First Vatican Council,* 23.

20. Ibid., 173.

21. O'Brien, *Isaac Hecker, An American Catholic,* 254.

22. Jay Dolan, *The American Catholic Experience* (Notre Dame/London: University of Notre Dame Press, 1992), 235–36.

23. Cited in O'Brien, *Isaac Hecker, An American Catholic,* 256.

24. Isaac Hecker, "Notes begun in Egypt in 1873," cited in John Farina, *An American Experience of God: The Spirituality of Isaac Hecker* (Ramsey, NJ: Paulist Press, 1981), 145.

25. O'Brien, *Isaac Hecker, An American Catholic,* 275; Farina, *American Experience of God,* 154–55.

26. O'Brien, *Isaac Hecker, An American Catholic,* 337.

27. Isaac Hecker, *The Church and the Age* (New York: Office of the Catholic World, 1887), 33.

28. Cited in O'Brien, *Isaac Hecker, An American Catholic,* 375.

6
VATICAN I (1869–1870)

Although Vatican I is frequently treated today as an essentially reactionary and defensive moment in the history of the Church, the council brought together several strands of ecclesiological thought and produced the fullest specifically ecclesiological conciliar text prior to Vatican II.

—Michael J. Himes[1]

"Vatican I was the Catholic answer to the *many* revolutions affecting the nineteenth century."[2] Among these revolutions we may count the American Revolution, the French Revolution, the Industrial Revolution, and the scientific revolution. Each in its own fashion created or caused problems for the church, and the council was *the* Catholic answer to these problems. There are those who interpret Vatican I with such a hermeneutic of suspicion that it seems to be an expression of "stifling despotism" on the part of Pio Nono and his cronies, "trying to get away with the dogma of papal infallibility."[3] To say the least, this is a most inadequate perception of the council.

The council opened on December 8, 1869, and suspended sessions on September 1, 1870. About eighty thousand people filed into St. Peter's Basilica for the opening ceremonies. At 8:30 a.m. the *Veni Creator* was intoned, and by 3:30 p.m. the ceremonies came to an end. About eight hundred cardinals, patriarchs, archbishops, bishops, abbots, and religious superiors participated. Poorer bishops and vicars apostolic from missionary territories, many of whom had been created by the pope, were lodged at Pius's own expense in Rome. This gave rise to Pius's witty remark, appreciated only in Italian: "I don't know whether the pope will emerge from this Council fallible or infallible *[fallibile od infallibile]*, but it is certain that he will be bankrupt *[fallito]*."⁴ This was the first general council of the church in which bishops assembled in Rome from every continent. It must be recalled that at the Council of Trent in the sixteenth century the world was still in the process of being opened up geographically. It is also interesting and of note that the presence and participation of English-speaking bishops in Vatican I was substantive, some 120 taking part.⁵ Again it is interesting that the heads of Catholic countries did not participate in any formal way, a clear recognition of what had occurred since the French Revolution—the separation of church and state.

Two doctrinal constitutions were promulgated, *Dei Filius* (April 24, 1870), dealing with reason and faith, and *Pastor Aeternus* (July 18, 1870), defining the primacy and infallibility of the pope. Thirty-five theologians were invited from outside Italy. Most of them were ultramontane in outlook, but Ignaz von Döllinger and John Henry Newman were far from ultramontanism. In fact, Döllinger was vetoed by the archbishop of Munich, Cardinal Reisach, and Newman did not accept the invitation for a number of reasons: his health, his dislike of ecclesiastical politics, and the fact that he was working on his book *An Essay in Aid of a Grammar of Assent*. While he was at work on his book, his fellow priest and former friend Henry Edward Manning was hard at work promoting a conciliar definition of papal infallibility.

Henry Edward Manning

The youngest son of William Manning, a member of parliament, Henry Edward Manning was educated at Harrow and Balliol College, Oxford. In 1832 he was elected to a fellowship at Merton College, Oxford, and was ordained a deacon. The following year he went as curate to John Sargent, rector of

Lavington. In May 1833 he succeeded Sargent as rector, and later that year he married Caroline, Sargent's daughter, but she died in 1837. In 1841 Manning became archdeacon of Chichester. Though originally an evangelical, he now allied himself with the Tractarians and authored No. 78 in the *Tracts for the Times*. After Newman became a Catholic in 1845, a number looked to Manning as a leader of the Oxford Movement. He was received into the Catholic Church in 1851, and two months later he was ordained a priest by Archbishop Nicholas Wiseman. In 1857, he was made provost of the Westminster Metropolitan Chapter, and he succeeded Wiseman as archbishop of Westminster in 1865.

Manning and Newman make an interesting contrast. "Manning's private and personal influence in his way and in his own day was just as great as Newman's, but as it belonged to the realm of deeds and to the spoken rather than the written word, so it died with those who had known him, whereas heart still speaks to heart wherever Newman finds readers."[6] Both had gone to Oxford, both had been Anglican priests, both were influential in the Church of England, and both became Catholics. Manning, however, thought Newman's brand of Catholicism dangerous. What he feared was "An English Catholicism of which Newman is the highest type. It is the old Anglican, patristic, literary, Oxford tone transplanted into the Church....It is worldly Catholicism." Newman's Catholicism, for Manning, was insufficiently certain and bold, not tailored enough to decisive, public action. Both believed in papal infallibility, but while Newman thought that a definition was both unnecessary and unwise and might discourage conversions to the Catholic Church, Manning was convinced that far from having an adverse reaction in England, such a definition would bring Anglicans flocking to Rome. What Manning wanted was "downright, masculine, and decided Catholics—*more* Roman than Rome, and more Ultramontane than the Pope himself."[7] For Manning, "Ultramontanism is Catholic Christianity."[8] As a man of action, he set himself wholeheartedly to do all in his power to achieve the highest expression of his ultramontanism through his promotion of the definition of papal infallibility.

Before returning to the Vatican Council, we get perhaps another insight into Manning by recalling that he shared a platform with none other than Francis Newman! On October 22, 1867, at a meeting in the Manchester Free Trade Hall, Francis Newman and Archbishop Manning found themselves sharing similar views on the social problems caused by alcohol. Manning knew the problems alcohol caused, not least among his large and growing Irish immigrant flock in London, and so he allied himself with the tirade of some fervent Protestants, including Francis Newman, "against the enormous excess of the trade in intoxicating drink." When Francis Newman wrote to his brother John about his enthusiasm for Manning on this issue, thinking this might be something both brothers shared in common, John replied: "'As to what you tell me of Archbishop Manning, I have heard that some also of our Irish bishops think that too many drink-shops are licensed. As for me, I do not know whether we have too many or too few.'"[9] This was not Francis's hoped-for reply. Newman knew about drink and its problems. He lived in industrial Birmingham, and his first church in that conurbation was in a former gin distillery.

Dei Filius

The initial sessions of the council were given over to the Dogmatic Constitution *Dei Filius,* which had to do with revelation and faith.[10] The *schema,* prepared largely by the Roman theologian Johannes Franzelin, SJ, was judged too long, too technical, and too hostile to the modern world and so was returned for revision. The revision was undertaken by another Roman theologian, Johannes Kleutgen, SJ, and eventually this was promulgated as the constitution *Dei Filius* on April 24, 1870.

The opening section of *Dei Filius* reiterates Christ's presence to and in the church, guarding and assisting the church into all truth. Chapter 1 is "On God the Creator of All Things." God is distinct from the world and creates not out of necessity, but freely, to manifest his perfection. Chapter 2 is "On Revelation." Its opening sentence reads: "The same holy mother Church holds and teaches that God, the source and end of all things, may be known [*cognosci posse*] with certainty from the consideration of created things, by the natural power of human reason...." This is a natural knowledge of God. The constitution goes on to insist that God has made himself known also in a "supernatural way," through the scriptures and lastly by his Son (Heb 1:1–2). Chapter 3 is "On Faith." Faith accepts what God reveals, and that acceptance is based not on "the natural light of reason" but on "the authority of God himself." Faith is a gift of God. The chapter also defends the reasonableness of the act of faith, insisting on this against the fideist tradition of Protestant pietism. Chapter 4 is "On Faith and Reason."

> Now reason, if it is enlightened by faith, does indeed when it seeks persistently, piously and soberly, achieve by God's gift some understanding, and that most fruitful, of the mysteries, whether by analogy from what it knows naturally, or from the *nexus* of these mysteries with one another and with the final end of humankind; but reason is never rendered capable of penetrating these mysteries in the way in which it penetrates those truths which form its proper object. For the divine mysteries, by their very nature, so far exceed the created understanding that, even when a revelation has been given and accepted in faith, they remain covered by the veil of that same faith and wrapped, as it were, in a certain obscurity, as long as in this mortal life "we are away from the Lord, for we walk by faith, and not by sight" (2 Cor 5:6–7).[11]

The conviction of the constitution is that since God is the source both of our intelligence/reason and revelation/faith, there can be no real disagreement between reason and faith. Rather, faith and reason are mutually supportive.

Pastor Aeternus

At least at the outset, there was no pressure on the council participants to rush through important matters and to steamroll toward the definition of papal infallibility. There was full and, from the comment of the participating bishops, sometimes frustratingly repetitious debate.

The *schema* on the church could have been much finer. The scholar of nineteenth-century theology Michael Himes points out: "The Roman School's incarnational ecclesiology laid the theological groundwork and colored the actual language of *Pastor Aeternus,* but unfortunately neither its patristic richness nor its systematic vision is reflected in the document."[12] The patristic richness owes something to the influence of Johann Adam Möhler on the Roman school of theology, but it was not to make its way into the actual text of the document. It was not only the theology of the document that was lacking in richness. The atmosphere among the prelates was quickly concentrated around papal infallibility. Different groups formed around the question of papal infallibility, with the majority, in fact, being in favor of some kind of definition of infallibility. Real debate took place, though it is not obvious from a cursory reading of the finished text of *Pastor Aeternus.* "The text as we have it fails to show any marks of the sweat— rather, stains of the blood—that was shed as it was being composed. *It is the product of a conflict between ecclesiologies."*[13]

Both in Rome and in the background were the extremist ultramontanes who advocated for the most comprehensive possible definition. William G. Ward, a convert from Anglicanism, for example, desired that all papal pronouncements be considered infallible. Some bishops came very close to sharing Ward's perspective, the most notable being Archbishop Manning of

Westminster, who used excessive language of the pope such as "the incarnation of the Holy Spirit." It was not only the bishops who entered the lists on the issue of papal authority. The French Catholic layman and ultramontane Louis Veuillot, editor of the paper the *Universe* wrote: "We all know certainly one thing, that is that no man knows anything except the man with whom God is for ever, the Man who carries through the thought of God. We must unswervingly follow his inspired directions." A hymn published in the *Universe* contains these words:

> To Pius IX, Pontiff-King:
> Father of the poor,
> Giver of Gifts,
> Light of hearts,
> Send forth the beam
> Of your heavenly light!

The Jesuit paper in Rome, *Civiltà Cattolica,* said: "When the Pope thinks, it is God who is thinking in him."[14] While leaving open the element of ecclesiological truth found in these expressions, this is surely hyperbole. These were the "infallibilists."

A minority group was opposed to defining infallibility at the council, the "anti-infallibilists." This group included many of the French bishops, headed by Archbishop Georges Darboy of Paris and Bishop Felix Dupanloup of Orleans. Margaret O'Gara describes Bishop Dupanloup's activities both before and at the council: "Before the council, Dupanloup had begun extensive correspondence with Rome, with other bishops, and with foreign theologians. Soon after arriving at Rome, he plunged into a series of feverish organizing activities, using his residence as a base of operations."[15] Dupanloup wrote to Pio Nono late in April 1870:

> Most Holy Father, My name is not pleasing to you; I know it, and it is my sorrow. But for all that, I feel myself authorized and obliged, in the profound and

inviolable devotion of which I have given so many proofs to Your Holiness, to open my heart to you at this moment....I would think I was betraying the Holy See and the Church if, knowing what I know, and foreseeing what I foresee, I did not utter a word of warning to Your Holiness...while there is yet time to spare the Church and the Holy See from evils that may become disasters for all Christendom during long ages....

Dupanloup, as well as the other French bishops, may not simply be disregarded as marked by a false, Gallican ecclesiology that expressed itself in bitter opposition to papal infallibility. They had the good of the church at heart, and from their perspective infallibility was the wrong course to take. This was a matter of conscience. Pius replied to Dupanloup early in May:

Venerable Brother, Your name is no less pleasing to us now than in the past, nor do we love you less, or esteem less than formerly the gifts that God has bestowed upon you....Return, brother, I pray you to that golden simplicity of little ones; cast away prejudiced opinions, which may obscure the holiness of your character, and which may make, if not pernicious, certainly useless for the Church those great gifts of intellect, alacrity, eloquence, with which God has so liberally endowed you for the extending of his Kingdom.[16]

The tone is somewhat patronizing, to be sure, but it is not without its kindness and concern, as much for Dupanloup himself as for the church.

The reasons for the French opposition are complex, but certainly important are the Gallican tendencies of the earlier nineteenth century, when most of the French bishops were in seminary. Gallicanism, by and large, exemplifies a certain pride in French Catholicism, advocating a decentralized church, with great respect for the independence of the local diocesan community. Some of these "Gallican" French bishops not only maintained their opposition to infallibility during the council's proceedings, but left Rome before the final vote was taken on July 18, so that they would not, in conscience, have to vote against it. Some American bishops sided with the French party also, most prominently Archbishop Kenrick of St. Louis. Then there were the "inopportunists," those who regarded it inopportune to promote a definition. Representative of this group was Archbishop Martin Spalding of Baltimore and many of the Austrian and German bishops.

Alec Vidler points out that there was ample opportunity for discussion of the matter at the council and that the inopportunists were not simply browbeaten into submission. He writes: "No doubt there was much intrigue behind the scenes, but no more than is customary, and perhaps inevitable, in ecclesiastical assemblies."[17] These are sage remarks. If we had a complete record of the proceedings of every church council, we would see in varying degrees similar intrigue, as the advocates of different theological positions made their positions clear and also tried to influence others. This is the way of conversation and debate, and there simply is no short-circuiting the process. Archbishop Manning gives us some idea of the intrigue behind the scenes. He tells us that the inopportunists "met often, and we met weekly to watch and counteract. When they went to Pius IX we went also. It was a running fight."[18] Eamon Duffy's judgment about these extreme infallibilists is surely accurate: "Manning and his associates wanted history without tears, a living oracle who could short-circuit human limitation. They wanted to confront the uncertainties of their age with instant assurance, revelation on tap."[19] As things turned out, the extreme infallibilists did not get what they wanted.

In early January 1870, the infallibilists got together five hundred signatures petitioning for a definition, since the original *schema* on the church did not explicitly include it. The opposition managed to get only 136 signatories for a counterpetition. As a result of the majority request, a chapter on infallibility was added to the *schema* on the church. A new constitution on the church, now including the definition of papal primacy and infallibility, was announced on April 29. Debate continued from May until the middle of July. The best theologian of the English episcopate, William Clifford, made a speech insisting that virtually any statement made by the council about papal authority was bound to cause some degree of misunderstanding unless it was presented within the more general framework of a statement on authority in the church as a whole. He was hissed at by some of the audience in the aula. On June 18, the Dominican theologian Cardinal Filippo Maria Guidi, archbishop of Bologna and an ardent infallibilist, made the emphatic point from the podium in the council aula that it was not the *pope* who was infallible but his teaching. He argued that a condition of infallibility was its prudent exercise, in consultation with the worldwide episcopate. Guidi himself was an infallibilist; however, he was keen to state the tradition that the pope was no isolated monarch, but rather was first among the bishops. When Guidi descended from the podium after his speech, he was embraced by members of the minority who appreciated his conciliatory perspective. Pius felt betrayed and summoned Guidi, and this is the famous occasion on which he said to him: "I am the Church! I am the tradition."[20]

The preamble to the actual text of *Pastor Aeternus* often is overlooked, and yet it is very important for an adequate interpretation of the decree, as Fergus Kerr, OP, comments: "The preamble of 'Pastor Aeternus' sets the doctrine touching the institution, perpetuity, and nature of the Petrine primacy very firmly in the context of preserving the unity of the episcopate within a Church which has been founded to perpetuate the saving work of redemption."[21] Chapters 1 and 2 of *Pastor Aeternus* define "a primacy of jurisdiction over the whole Church of God," given to St. Peter and to his successors, the popes. This primacy of jurisdiction is "over all others" in matters of faith and morals, and also in matters of discipline and government. As it stands, this kind of language suggests that the bishops are nothing more than papal representatives. In chapter 3 of the document, however, we read:

> So far is this power of the pope from being damaging or obstructive to that ordinary and immediate power of episcopal jurisdiction by which bishops, who have been set by the Holy Spirit to succeed and hold the place of the Apostles, feed and govern each his own flock, as true pastors, that their power, precisely, is asserted, strengthened and protected by the supreme and universal pastor.

In other words, the bishops are not mere papal mouthpieces but succeed to the place of the apostles, and the pope's role is to assert, strengthen, and protect the pastorate of the bishops. The understanding of papal primacy is that its role is to maintain and support and never to weaken or threaten the integrity of local churches.

In terms of papal infallibility, a formula on its nature and extent that came from Cardinal Paul Cullen of Dublin, who had nominated Newman as rector of the Catholic University, was finally accepted by a majority of the conciliar fathers. This formula fell short of what the more rigorous ultramontanes wanted. Nonetheless, it won the day and was incorporated into the constitution, *Pastor Aeternus,* which was adopted formally on July 18 by a vote of 433 to 2.

It is in chapter 4 that we find the definition of infallibility.

> We teach and define as a divinely revealed dogma that when the Roman Pontiff speaks from the chair *(ex cathedra),* that is, when, in the exercise of his office as shepherd and teacher of all Christians, in virtue of his supreme apostolic authority, he defines a doctrine concerning faith or morals to be held by the whole Church, he possesses, by the divine assistance promised him in blessed Peter, that infallibility which the

divine Redeemer willed his Church to enjoy in defining doctrine concerning faith or morals. Therefore, such definitions of the Roman Pontiff are of themselves, and not by the consent of the church, irreformable.

The definition is complex and sounds very strong indeed, almost giving the pope free rein in matters doctrinal and moral. It demands some theological comment by way of clarification. The last sentence, "Therefore, such definitions…irreformable," is couched in this way to reject the position adopted by the 1682 assembly of French bishops, the Gallican Articles. These articles insist that for definitions of the pope to be binding they must have the consequent assent of the church. The concordat with Napoleon in 1801 added another strand to this Gallicanism. The clergy of France, now salaried by the government and thus to some extent controlled by the government, were caught in the tension between national interests and the international interests of the church. One historian draws the conclusion: "It was these political conditions that necessitated the dogma of papal infallibility for the same reason that the political conditions of the eleventh century necessitated the papal decree on lay investiture: The liberty of the Church was at stake."[22]

Here in the text of *Pastor Aeternus* the implication seems to be that such *consequent* assent is unnecessary since the *prior* consultation with the episcopate would have taken place, thus making consequent assent redundant. It was generally assumed that no pope would proceed with an infallible definition without consulting the church, as in fact Pope Pius IX had done prior to his definition of the dogma of the Immaculate Conception of the Blessed Virgin Mary in 1854. As E. E. Y. Hales wrote: "It was, indeed unthinkable that [the pope] should do otherwise. But no wording to this effect was put into the definition."[23]

Theological clarification from the pen of F. X. Lawlor in the former edition of the *New Catholic Encyclopedia* (and reissued in the enlarged second edition) is especially clear on this

111

important point. Lawlor writes: "The pope's juridic autonomy does not entail discommunity or isolation; his juridic independence is never a solitary independence. He always acts as part of the Body, in the sense that he acts from within a metajuridic community of life, based on the fact that the Spirit assumes a continuum of faith both lived and taught between the Roman Pontiff and his fellow believers in the Church and his fellow bishops in the episcopate."[24] Critics of papal infallibility point to the fact that this way of understanding is not formally explicit in the text of *Pastor Aeternus*. While that may be true, the theological datum and context explicated by Lawlor, and indeed accepted probably by the majority of Catholic ecclesiologists, give a sense of balance. Without this balancing context, papal infallibility loses its fundamental raison d'être, service of the church.

The Promulgation *of* Pastor Aeternus

The Rev. Thomas Mozley, Anglican priest, brother-in-law of Newman, and correspondent for the London *Times*—and, moreover, who knew no Italian or French and was dependent on hearsay for most of his reportage—describes the thunderstorm during which the vote was taken on *Pastor Aeternus:*

> The storm, which had been threatening all the morning, burst now with the utmost violence, and to many a superstitious mind might have conveyed the idea that it was an expression of divine wrath, as "no doubt it will be interpreted by numbers," said one officer of the Palatine Guard. And so the "placets" [positive votes] of the fathers struggled through the storm, while the thunder pealed above and the lightning flashed in at every window and down through the

dome and every smaller cupola, dividing if not absorbing the attention of the crowd. "Placet," shouted his Eminence or his Grace, and a loud clap of thunder followed in response, and then the lightning darted about the baldachino and every part of the church and the conciliar hall, as if announcing the response.[25]

Critics took this as a sign of God's anger. Not Archbishop Manning, who said, "They forgot Sinai and the Ten Commandments."[26]

Sixty-one fathers submitted written protests against the definitions and left Rome on the eve of the solemn promulgation, though they accepted it once it had been passed. The two bishops who voted against it, Luigi Riccio of Caiazzo, Italy, and Edward Fitzgerald of Little Rock, Arkansas, accepted the definitions right away.

Conclusion

The day following the definition of infallibility, war was declared between Prussia and France, effectively bringing the council prematurely to an end. The French needed all their military, and so the French garrison in Rome, guaranteeing papal independence and protection, was withdrawn almost immediately. Within a month King Victor Emmanuel invaded the Papal States. Rome fell to his troops on September 20, and Pius became the "prisoner of the Vatican." On October 20 Pio Nono issued an apostolic letter suspending the council indefinitely.

No bishop left the church over the papal definitions. By the end of 1870, almost all the French bishops who had opposed infallibility had accepted it, and had signified that acceptance by letter to the pope, by a pastoral letter, or by some other means of promulgating the conciliar decree in their individual dioceses.[27] Dom Cuthbert Butler says of the anti-infallibilist bishops, "It is not to be supposed that the submission of faith came automatically or easily.... There was a period of hesitation and interior struggle and conflict, that had to be battled through, before catholic principle came out victorious over private judgment."[28] While extreme ultramontanists like Archbishop Manning sought the most aggressive interpretation of *Pastor Aeternus,* not every bishop thought or acted in this way. The English bishops, for example, did not issue a joint pastoral letter on Vatican I until their Low Week meeting of 1875. What they came up with on that occasion was essentially an endorsement of the Declaration of the German Episcopate. The English bishops' pastoral letter balanced Vatican I's position on the papacy with an acknowledgment of the rights of local bishops. A bishop was not simply a papal vicar.

Although no bishop left, a number of theologians were excommunicated or left the church. The German theologian Johann Friedrich left the church over it and with his followers formed the schismatic group known as the Old Catholics. Ignaz Döllinger, the German theologian, historian, and friend of the late Johann Adam Möhler, could not accept the definition of infallibility, despite the gentle encouragement and sensitivity of his ordinary, Archbishop Gregor von Scherr of Munich, and incurred excommunication.

It is sometimes suggested that Pope Pius IX promised preferment to those who engineered and lobbied for the definition of papal infallibility, but this seems most implausible. No one was made a cardinal for three years after the council, and then it was roughly equal between pro- and anti-infallibilist bishops. Archbishop Manning, for example, "to whom the Pope was most indebted, and who had succeeded Cardinal Wiseman in 1865 as Archbishop of Westminster, was not elevated to the purple until 1875."[29]

In the wake of Vatican II there have been various reappraisals of Vatican I, not all of equal value. The work of August Hasler is probably the most severe and bitter attack on papal infallibility in recent times. In 1979 he published a shorter

English version of a two-volume work in German, *How the Pope Became Infallible: Pius IX and the Politics of Persuasion.*[30] Hasler doubted the truth of the standard histories of Vatican I, especially when dealing with *Pastor Aeternus.* His own work points up the manipulative techniques of Pio Nono and suggests that the pope had extremely severe mental health challenges. The net result was Pius's undue pressure on the council fathers, who really were not free to conduct their business. The lack of freedom made the conciliar decree invalid. On the positive side, Hasler did have access to the private notes of conciliar participants, especially those of Archbishop Darboy of Paris. These would be expected to throw new light on the proceedings. But to undermine the performance of the majority at the council who advocated the definition in some way or another, based often on an unscholarly analysis of their psychological state, is a strange way to do history.

On the other hand, the Irish Jesuit theologian and ecumenist Patrick O'Connell is far more accurate and even-handed when he writes: "The manner in which papal primacy has been expressed and in which it has exercised its functions has been culturally conditioned."[31] It is to this cultural conditioning of papal primacy that Pope John Paul II refers when, in his encyclical letter *Ut Unum Sint,* he invites ecumenical dialogue on the matter. O'Connell goes on to say that episcopal collegiality and papal primacy must be understood together, rather than in some kind of competition: "Vatican II in its teaching on episcopal collegiality reveals not so much the other side of the coin of Vatican I as the full face of the coin. The truth is not primacy balanced by collegiality but primacy in collegiality."[32] It is the working out of this primacy in collegiality that is one of the key issues in ecclesiology today—and, indeed, has been since 1870. It is here that dispute and debate hold sway, but there can be no dispute about O'Connell's conclusion concerning not only the Petrine ministry but the exercise of any authority in the church. "When all authority in the Church is basically service of the brethren, following the example of

Christ the Lord, what is the real difference between presidency or primacy of honor and primacy of jurisdiction?"[33] Placing the accent on authority as service does not solve immediately all the contentious issues concerning the Petrine ministry that arose out of Vatican I, but a fuller understanding of the primacy of service offers nothing but hope.

Bibliography

Butler, Cuthbert, OSB. *The Vatican Council.* 2 vols. London/New York: Longmans Green, 1930.

Duffy, Eamon. *Saints and Sinners: A History of the Popes. Rev. ed.* New Haven/London: Yale University Press, 2001.

O'Gara, Margaret. *Triumph and Defeat: Infallibility, Vatican I and the French Minority Bishops.* Washington, DC: Catholic University of America Press, 1988.

Notes

1. Michael J. Himes, "The Development of Ecclesiology: Modernity to the Twentieth Century," in *The Gift of the Church,* ed. Peter C. Phan (Collegeville, MN: Liturgical Press, 2000), 61.

2. Joseph Fitzer, *Romance and the Rock: Nineteenth Century Catholics on Faith and Reason* (Minneapolis: Augsburg Press, 1989), 5.

3. E. E. Y. Hales, *Pio Nono* (New York: J. Kenedy & Sons, 1954), 293.

4. Ibid., 295.

5. Ibid., 296.

6. Sheridan Gilley, "Newman and the Convert Mind," in *Newman and Conversion,* ed. Ian Ker (Notre Dame, IN: University of Notre Dame Press, 1997), 8.

7. Cited in Adrian Hastings, *A History of English Christianity 1920–1990* (London: Collins, 1986), 147.

8. J. Pereiro, *Cardinal Manning* (Oxford: Oxford University Press, 1964), 255.

9. Cited in Basil Willey, *More Nineteenth Century Studies* (New York: Harper and Row, 1966), 47.

10. A useful commentary on *Dei Filius* may be found in Gerald A. McCool, SJ, *Catholic Theology in the Nineteenth Century* (New York: Seabury Press, 1977), 216–40.

11. Translations from the Latin texts of *Dei Filius* and *Pastor Aeternus* are my own.

12. Himes, "Development of Ecclesiology," 61.

13. Fergus Kerr, OP, "Vatican I and the Papacy 1: A Proud Appellation," *New Blackfriars* 60 (1979): 170. This is the first in a series of superb essays by Kerr on Vatican I and the Papacy that I have found to be especially helpful. This first essay covers pp. 164–76, and the others are "2: Conditions for an Orthodox Pope" (pp. 196–206); "3: The Attitude of the English Bishops" (pp. 257–69); "4: The Conflict between the English Bishops" (pp. 335–47); "5: Defining 'Defining,'" (pp. 356–66); "6: The Question of Infallibility" (pp. 404–16); "7: Reception and Revision" (pp. 452–64); "8: Recent Catholic Approaches," *New Blackfriars* 61 (1980): 24–34.

14. These citations are from Margaret O'Gara, *Triumph in Defeat: Infallibility, Vatican I, and the French Minority Bishops* (Washington, DC: Catholic University of America Press, 1988), 70.

15. Ibid., 31.

16. Cuthbert Butler, OSB, *The Vatican Council* (London/New York: Longmans, Green, 1930), 2:40–42.

17. Alec R. Vidler, *The Church in an Age of Revolution,* rev. ed. (Harmondsworth: Penguin Books, 1974), 156.

18. E. R. Purcell, *Life of Cardinal Manning* (New York/London: Macmillan, 1896), 2:453.

19. Duffy, *Saints and Sinners,* 299.

20. Butler, *Vatican Council,* 2:96–98.

21. Kerr, "Vatican I and the Papacy 1," 169.

22. Thomas Bokenkotter, *A Concise History of the Catholic*

Church, revised and expanded edition (New York: Doubleday, 2004), 326.

23. Hales, *Pio Nono,* 309.

24. F. X. Lawlor and others, "Infallibility," *New Catholic Encyclopedia,* 2nd ed. (Detroit: Thomson/Gale in association with The Catholic University of America, 2003), 7:450.

25. Cited in Butler, *Vatican Council,* 2:163.

26. Cited in Duffy, *Saints and Sinners,* 301.

27. Butler, *Vatican Council,* 2:171.

28. Ibid., 2:187.

29. Hales, *Pio Nono,* 312.

30. August Hasler, *How the Pope Became Infallible: Pius IX and the Politics of Persuasion* (New York: Crossroad, 1981).

31. Patrick O'Connell, SJ, "Papal Primacy Then and Now," in *Irish Anglicanism 1869–1969,* ed. Michael Hurley, SJ (Dublin: Allen Figgis, 1970), 208.

32. Ibid., 204.

33. Ibid., 210.

7
POPE LEO XIII (1810–1903)

Ideologically, Leo XIII does not stand among the extremists. He was neither a reactionary, nor by any means a doctrinaire liberal. Perhaps the more neutral term "progressive" best characterizes him.

—Raymond H. Schmandt[1]

Gioacchino Vincenzo Pecci (1810–1903), born in Carpineto in central Italy, received his doctorate in theology in 1832 from the Roman College (the Gregorian University), went on to receive further credentials from the Roman Academy for Noble Ecclesiastics and the Sapienza University. He was ordained a priest on December 31, 1837, and his first diplomatic post took him to Benevento in the Papal States from 1838 to 1841. He had a similar post in Perugia, the capital of Umbria, for one year and then, having been consecrated titular archbishop of Damietta, the thirty-three-year-old archbishop was sent to Belgium as papal nuncio in 1843. His three years there, though not free of problems with the prime minister, Nothomb, were to shape his outlook as pope. These years introduced him to industrial northern Europe with all its gifts and problems and also forced him to think more openly about liberal, democratic regimes. The diplomatic difficulties he encountered brought about his withdrawal from Brussels and his return to Perugia, but now as archbishop, and he remained until his election as pope in 1878.

Pecci's temperament was conservative and in Perugia he promoted a small-scale version, through a pastoral letter, of Pio Nono's *Syllabus of Errors*. His brother, Joseph, was a Jesuit seminary professor, and it was largely through him that Pecci became interested in Thomism as the preferred way of philosophical and theological reflection in the church. He established the Academy of St. Thomas Aquinas in Perugia to promote scholasticism. At Vatican I, Pecci voted with the majority in favor of infallibility, but Cardinal Giacomo Antonelli, Pio Nono's secretary of state, was suspicious of his openness to the modern world and kept him pretty much out of Rome itself. An indication of Pecci's openness to modern civilization emerges in his Lenten pastoral of 1877, "The Church and Civilization":

> Society, then, being composed of men essentially capable of improvement, cannot stand still; it advances and perfects itself. One age inherits the inventions, discoveries and improvements achieved by the preceding one, and thus the sum of physical, moral and political blessings can increase most marvelously.[2]

Such sentiments would not endear him to Antonelli in the wake of the taking of the Papal States, even though Pecci took Pio Nono's position on the Roman question. Despite his conservative temperament, Pecci was seen to be on the side of the progressives in the church.

The conclave of 1878 was by no means unanimous in voting for Cardinal Pecci. It was said that Pio Nono, still much revered among the cardinals, most of whom he had appointed, favored Cardinal Luigi Bilio as his successor. Bilio was a conservative and the primary author of Pio Nono's *Syllabus of Errors*. Even Cardinal Manning, archbishop of Westminster, was rumored as *papabile*. Owen Chadwick comments laconically on Manning: "There was irresponsible talk of electing Cardinal Manning of Westminster, who had made such a name as an ultramontane in the Vatican Council. Manning would have made an unsatisfactory pope."[3] Pecci seemed a more promising candidate all round and received the required two-thirds majority. Among the factors that probably led to Leo's election was the fact that he had authored a series of pastoral letters in his diocese of Perugia, from 1874 to 1877, that seemed to overcome the alienation between the church and the world and to promote a greater harmony. As Eamon Duffy has it, "It was time for a little sweet talk."[4]

As Pope Leo XIII, he seemed like a breath of fresh air in the church after the pontificate of Pope Pius IX, though the contrast between them can be exaggerated. Like his predecessor, Leo also had a long pontificate, lasting twenty-five years. Alec Vidler sums him up in these words: "He did mean to give the Church a new look. He was a great diplomat, and by temperament an optimist. Instead of emphasizing the alienation between the Church and the modern world, he wanted to convince the modern world that it needed the Church and that the Church was no longer sadly aspiring after a restoration of the *ancien régime.*"[5] Leo did away with the eunuchs, or castrati, who sang in the Sistine Chapel. The fact that the Vatican Council had not formally been closed in 1870 meant that the furniture for the bishops in council still existed, "just in case," but Leo gave instructions for the benches to be broken up. Whether he liked it personally or not, he recognized that there was little real hope of reconvening the council.

Leo XIII was "a man of encyclicals."[6] The encyclical letter in its modern form began with Pope Benedict XIV in 1740. Leo issued more encyclical letters than any pope before him. It was his favored medium of communicating with the church, and indeed with the wider world. The encyclicals covered virtually everything—socialism, scripture, the nature of philosophy, the unity of the church, Anglican orders, and so forth. Eamon Duffy writes with accuracy: "Here, for the first time, we have the Pope as an inexhaustible source of guidance and instruction. No pope before or since has come anywhere near his eighty-six encyclicals. Leo taught and taught, and expected obedience."[7]

Relationally, Pius IX and Leo XIII make an interesting contrast, according to the reactions and sentiments of their peers. People felt that when they talked to Pius he cared for them at that moment more than for anyone else in the world. Leo, on the other hand, was "cool, formal and courteous."[8]

French Catholics and Royalism

France in the 1880s saw church and state constantly in conflict. Many Catholics dreamed of a royalist return. The French republic saw disloyalty in such dreaming, and perhaps even treachery. Leo addressed himself to the French situation. In 1884, he published an encyclical with the title *The Most Noble Nation of the French,* and in this document, he praised the Concordat of 1801 and encouraged Catholics to lay aside extreme political views for the sake of the country. The following year he put out an encyclical on the nature of the state, which insisted that the church did not privilege any particular form of government, and he encouraged Catholics fully to participate in the social and political life of the state.

In October 1890 he summoned the premier liberal French bishop, Cardinal Charles Lavigerie, archbishop of Algiers, to make him his ally in the promotion of his policies. Consequent upon this meeting, Lavigerie invited the officers of the French fleet to a banquet on November 12 in which the cardinal proposed a toast pledging allegiance to the French republic. Moreover, as his guests were received, the band of the cardinal's missionary order, the White Fathers, played the "Marseillaise," an anthem identified with republicanism and *anathema* to the Catholic right. Lavigerie's toast, with Leo's full support, opened the floodgates of controversy in France. Leo's openness on these issues did not commend him to an influential number of the hierarchy who saw hope for the church only in the return of royalism. "His effort at reconciliation with a democracy did not succeed because his clergy and laity took their hats off to what he said but were no more reconciled to the republic than before."[9]

Capitalism, Social Justice, and Rerum Novarum

The nineteenth century witnessed the development of thinking on principles of social justice and the duties of capitalists to their workers, not least through the reflection of Karl Marx and Friedrich Engels. In the churches of northern Europe there was a growing concern among some Christians about the situation of the working class. Europe in the mid-nineteenth century threw up a number of thinkers who considered pressing questions of social change such as the elimination of poverty and the introduction of universal literacy and education, and the consequent raising of economic and living standards. Less well known are the *Christian Socialists,* a term introduced in 1848 in England. Better known are some Catholic thinkers and leaders whose concerns and commitment crossed the divide between ultramontane and liberal.

Wilhelm von Ketteler, the liberal bishop of Mainz, had been an opponent of the conciliar definition of papal infallibility but later accepted the definition. He was constantly concerned with the relationship between workers and the church. He had read with some degree of sympathy Karl Marx's *Das Kapital* on his way to the First Vatican Council and, though he disagreed with much of it, he nevertheless realized pragmatically that to engage in a realistic way with the problems of the working class, some measure of profit sharing had to be introduced. Though Ketteler died the year before Leo's election, his influence could still be felt. Similarly, though ultramontane rather than liberal, Cardinal Manning of Westminster became an advocate of social reform and was a leader in the settlement of the London dock strike of 1889.

Leon Harmel (1829–1915), an ultramontane French industrialist and capitalist, initiated a series of social and economic benefits for his workers and tried to promote such policies among other Catholic capitalists. He turned his textile plant near

Rheims into a Christian corporation under the patronage of Our Lady of the Factory. In 1887, he went to Rome on pilgrimage with one hundred employers, fourteen hundred employees, and three hundred priests. In 1889 his pilgrimage of workers numbered ten thousand. Eamon Duffy writes: "These pilgrimages of working people, living proof that democracy and the pope might shake hands, caught Leo's imagination, and helped persuade him that industrial society need not be conflictual, that social peace under the Gospel was a possibility."[10] The work and reflection of this growing body of Catholic social thinkers provided the ambiance for Leo's great encyclical, *Rerum Novarum,* of 1891.

Although *Rerum Novarum* condemned socialism, it tapped into the desire and the need for social and economic change. It insisted on the God-given right to private property, yes, but Leo also warned of the dangers of laissez-faire capitalism that "treats persons as atomized individuals and not as creatures in community."[11] The encyclical gave attention to the rights and the needs of workers, to their dignity, to the right of states to promote social justice, to the right of workers to form unions, and to their right to a decent, living wage and a share of profits. Strikes should generally be avoided, maintained Leo, but some may be justified in a fashion similar to the justification of self-defense. Owen Chadwick comments on the encyclical: "In the long view this encyclical made possible the Catholic social democratic parties of the twentieth century in Italy, Germany and Belgium and at moments in France."[12] *Rerum Novarum* was not in itself a radical document; indeed, some of its language could be construed as paternalistic and perhaps even romanticist, but for the pope to say such things after the long adversarial pontificate of Pius IX was "truly revolutionary."[13]

Theology and Scripture

"Theology had suffocated under Pio Nono."[14] One of the first things that Leo did was to make John Henry Newman a cardinal, lifting forever the cloud of suspicion that had hung over him. It is reported that Cardinal Manning of Westminster often said that Newman was a heretic. Leo's action put an end to that kind of calumny once and for all. It needs to be remembered that, although Newman had prepared for the priesthood in Rome at the Propaganda College, he was not of the Roman schools. His theological formation had been at Oxford, a significantly different milieu from Roman scholasticism. When Leo made Newman a cardinal, implicitly he was honoring a certain limited pluralism in Catholic theology.

Nonetheless, as pope, Leo privileged the thought of St. Thomas Aquinas as he had done earlier as archbishop of Perugia, and in his encyclical *Aeterni Patris* (1879), he called for a renewal of Thomistic philosophy and theology. In this he was influenced by his brother, now Cardinal Joseph Pecci, noted above, as well as by Fr. Matteo Liberatore. "A pope who loved the Middle Ages and wished to revive their impact in the modern world tried to make the supreme exponent of a medieval philosophy the only reliable exponent of modern philosophy."[15] This is the judgment of Owen Chadwick, and it may be challenged in part, but there is no doubt of its substantial truth. The Roman Academy of St. Thomas was reorganized in 1886, and Desire Mercier (1851–1926), later cardinal-archbishop of Malines, was nominated to a chair of Thomism at Louvain in 1882. Mercier insisted on teaching some philosophy courses in the vernacular so as "to bring the Scholastic mind within closer hailing distance of modern philosophers and their distinctive problems."[16] In 1889, with papal support, Mercier created the Institut Superieur de Philosophie, providing a complete education in the philosophical disciplines around and in engagement with the philosophy of St. Thomas. No one would deny the importance of Aquinas or of Thomism in the history of theology, nor their particular importance in the Catholic Church. The contemporary renaissance of interest in Aquinas evidences the constancy of his appeal and the ongoing significance of his thought. Nevertheless, it seems fair to say that Leo regarded

Thomism "not as the starting point of theological reflection, but as the *end of it*."[17] This seems to be part of the reason for the condemnation in 1887 of certain ideas and propositions of Antonio Rosmini-Serbati (1797–1855), a thinker who had considerable influence in northern Italy. Rosmini-Serbati was an encyclopedic thinker with at least initially an appreciation of Aquinas, but he sought to develop a system of thought that was organic and interlocking, that would serve as the basis of all knowledge. He went beyond Aquinas, taking account of modern philosophy. Forty propositions, taken out of context from all Rosmini's works, were condemned under Leo in 1887. Rosmini's disciples insisted at the time that these propositions did not genuinely represent his thought, and the Holy See has recently confirmed their position.[18]

In 1893, Leo issued his encyclical *Providentissimus Deus,* promoting the scholarly study of scripture among Catholics, especially the study of Oriental languages and the emerging techniques of biblical criticism. In that encyclical he wrote to Catholic students of scripture: "None of the recent discoveries which the human mind has made is foreign to the purpose of their work. On the contrary, let them make haste in any case where our times have discovered something useful in the matter of biblical exegesis to avail themselves of it forthwith and by their writings to put it at the service of all."[19] Nine years later, in 1902, he set up the Pontifical Biblical Commission. The late Jesuit theologian and ecumenist Gustave Weigel, wrote of this commission: "After [Leo's] death the Commission acted more as a brake than accelerator on biblical studies, but this was by reason of the rash temper of those times."[20] Weigel is referring to the consequent *debacle* of modernism, which will be discussed in a later chapter. In 1890, the Dominicans, under Père Marie-Joseph Lagrange, established the *École Biblique et Archéoloque Française de Jérusalem.* Within two years of the school's opening, the famous *Revue Biblique* began to appear.[21] Thus, we see something of a leap forward both in theology and in scripture during Leo's pontificate.

In 1879, Leo nominated Cardinal Josef Hergenroether as prefect of the Vatican Archives. Hergenroether was a pupil of Ignaz Döllinger (who had left the church after the definition of papal infallibility of Vatican I) and "one of the worst lecturers in Germany, droning away behind a high pile of books…and incapable of communicating any feeling for the past as alive."[22] Yet he was a good historian and had a feel for archival research. Slowly things began to move. In 1881, Leo opened the Vatican Archives to the historians of the world, much to the consternation of the Roman curia, noting, "We have nothing to fear from the publication of the documents."[23] To the scholarly community, this was a real breath of fresh air in contrast to what had happened in the previous pontificate.

Americanism

The American Catholic Church during Leo's pontificate might be characterized, in very general terms, as both insular-conservative and open-progressive. The insular part of the church, instanced in Archbishop Michael Corrigan of New York and German-American Catholic bishops especially in the Midwest, were somewhat suspicious of American nationalism and assimilation and wished to see Catholics withdraw from the state system in education and set up their own. The open part of the church, characterized by Cardinal James Gibbons of Baltimore and Archbishop John Ireland of St. Paul, argued for ongoing Catholic participation in the state system and the general assimilation of Catholic immigrants to American institutions and ideals. The positions of both camps were further colored by personal animosities.[24]

In 1891, Walter Elliott wrote a biography of Fr. Isaac Hecker, the convert founder of the Paulist Fathers. Hecker gave expression to a vibrant incarnational theology and outlook that seemed tailor-made, as it were, for the optimism of the flourishing United States of America. America was, of course, the birth

child of the Enlightenment, based on liberty, equality, and fraternity. Hecker's theology has been well characterized: "[His]
incarnational emphasis gave his ecclesiology an anthropologi-
cal orientation and his elevated appreciation of human nature
a theological foundation....He argued that man, heir to the
accumulated wisdom of the past and equipped with new freedom, was better prepared than ever to respond to a greater out-
pouring of the Holy Spirit."[25] It was all rather different from
recent European Catholic experience of liberty, equality, and
fraternity, most especially in France. In his introduction to the
biography, Archbishop Ireland praised Hecker as just the kind
of priest the modern world needed.

The biography was adapted and translated into French by
French Catholics allied to the cause of the French republic.
Hecker was their man too, and it caused quite a stir in France.
Those French churchmen opposed to the republic, and opposed
to the Hecker biography as a seeming support for cooperation
with that republic, created "Americanism." Americanism was
seen as the cumulative concessions of Catholics to modern
views, to freedom and tolerance, to accommodation to the modern state and modern culture. Royalist French Catholics saw it
as the very antithesis of Catholicism, that is, the countercultural
Catholicism that they espoused. The ensuing controversies and
debates came to the attention of Leo, who wrote the letter *Testem
Benevolentiae* in 1898 to Cardinal Gibbons and the American
hierarchy. Therein, having listed a number of ideas supposedly
associated with Fr. Hecker (e.g., undue emphasis on the inner
guidance of the Holy Spirit, minimizing the need for "external"
spiritual direction, emphasizing the active life over the contemplative life), he wrote:

> We cannot approve the opinions which some comprise
> under the head of Americanism. If indeed by that
> name be designated characteristic qualities which
> reflect honor on the people of America, conditions of
> your commonwealth, or the laws and customs which

prevail in them, there is surely no reason why we should deem it should be discarded. But, if it is to be used not only to signify but even to commend the above doctrines, there can be no doubt that our Venerable Brethren the bishops of America would be the first to repudiate and condemn it, as being especially unjust to them and to the entire nation as well. For it raises the suspicion that there are some among you who conceive of and desire a church in America different from that which is in the rest of the world.[26]

No condemnation and no penalty were issued against anyone, and the pope assured his American fellow bishops in the section of the letter cited that he did not believe that the bishops held any of the positions he had listed. Cardinal Gibbons rightly said in respect of the letter that no educated American Catholic held the ideas condemned in it, but damage had been done.[27] "Americanism" was something of a phantom heresy, pointing up the bitter divisions between the insular-conservative style of Catholicism with the more open-progressive style.

It may be, in part, that Cardinal Gibbons's own participation in the Parliament of World's Religions in Chicago in 1892 paved the way for this condemnation. All religions were presented in the parliament on an equal basis. That does not mean, of course, that Gibbons and other Catholics who participated understood Catholicism as on a par with other faiths, but their very participation itself left them open to that criticism on the part of their opponents. Whatever its roots and causes, the condemnation of Americanism had a negative effect on American Catholic theology and served as a harbinger for the condemnation of modernism in the next pontificate.[28]

In a letter of 1902 to Cardinal Gibbons and the American bishops, Leo wrote: "Therefore, while the changes and tendencies of nearly all the nations which were Catholic for many centuries give cause for sorrow, the state of your churches, in their flourishing youthfulness, cheers our heart and fills it with delight." Archbishop John Ireland quoted Leo as saying of America, "*L'avvenire*—'The Future.'"[29]

Relations with Other Christians

Leo had a considerable interest in Christian reunion. This may have been motivated by the hope that such a reunion would provide a stronger defense of the Christian faith in the face of increasing secularism. Of course, given the times, his model of ecumenism was the return of other ecclesial traditions and bodies to union with Rome and the Holy See. Leo was especially interested in reunion with the Oriental and Slavic churches, encouraged in this by Bishop Josip Strossmayer (1815–1905), the Croat bishop of Djakovo. Strossmayer, who had been a leading opponent of the definition of papal infallibility at Vatican I but afterwards accepted the conciliar decision, was a great advocate of church unity among the Russian Slavic peoples.

While in Belgium as nuncio, Leo had met Fr. Ignatius Spencer, an English convert and Passionist priest, and his conversations with Spencer seem to have been his entrée to English affairs. En route from Brussels to Rome in 1846, Pecci spent about a month in England, studying its political institutions, during which time he dined with Queen Victoria and attended a session of parliament. He knew something of English church affairs, but not a great deal.

In 1890 two men were vacationing on the island of Madeira—the Frenchman Abbé Fernand Portal and the Englishman Lord Halifax. Halifax was a high Anglican, with a high ecclesiology and theology of the sacraments. Portal was mightily impressed with Halifax's account of Anglican belief and practice. As a consequence of their conversations, both during the vacation and afterwards, both men gave serious attention to the question of the reunion of Canterbury and Rome. Portal wrote a brief pamphlet on Anglican orders, reaching a positive conclusion, and this was endorsed by one of the greatest French scholars of the time, Abbé Louis Duchesne. Duchesne's endorsement gave the question of Anglican orders high profile indeed. All was not well, however, with this incipient exercise in ecumenical relations. On the one hand, Abbé Portal did not sufficiently appreciate the complexity of the English church, and certainly not that Halifax's party of high Anglicans constituted numerically not a very large percentage of the Church of England. On the other hand, Cardinal Herbert Vaughan, archbishop of Westminster, was quite opposed to any kind of *rapprochement* on this matter of Anglican orders. "While [Vaughan] supported the proposed reinvestigation into the validity of Anglican orders, he suspected that it would be of very doubtful help in any way to reunion. To his mind such a reunion quite transcended any decision about orders and was, in fact, unlikely to come about in the foreseeable future."[30] Vaughan also did not like the suggestion that corporate reunion might put off individual conversions of Anglicans. Equally, Archbishop Edward White Benson of Canterbury did not take well to the speculation that Anglican orders needed any kind of recognition of their validity by Rome—or by any other body for that matter.

The entire issue was enormously complicated not only in theological terms but also in terms of personalities, past history, and ecclesiological presuppositions. Eventually, a papal commission was appointed in 1895 to study Anglican orders. An apostolic letter, *Apostolicae Curae,* was issued in 1896 condemning the orders as "null and void," both in form and in intention: "We pronounce and declare that ordinations performed according to the Anglican Rite have been and are completely null and void."[31] Even as this chapter is being written, however, Cardinal Walter Kasper of the Pontifical Council for Christian Unity suggests that new approaches toward a more positive understanding of Anglican orders are being thought through.

Conclusion

Leo XIII was no extremist. In some ways he has very close to Pio Nono, and yet in other ways he was more open to modernity and to modern ways in theology and the church. He is best understood as "progressive," his contribution to the church being "a subtle alloy of flexibility and obduracy."[32] Under him the papacy recovered something of its prestige and role of leadership in the world.

Bibliography

Chadwick, Owen. *A History of the Popes 1830–1914.* Oxford: Clarendon Press, 1998.

Duffy, Eamon. *Saints and Sinners: A History of the Popes. Rev. ed.* New Haven/London: Yale University Press, 2001.

Gargan, Edward T., ed. *Leo XIII and the Modern World.* New York: Sheed and Ward, 1961.

Notes

1. Raymond H. Schmandt, "The Life and Work of Leo XIII," in *Leo XIII and the Modern World,* ed. Edward T. Gargan (New York: Sheed and Ward, 1961), 35.

2. Cited from Raymond H. Schmandt, "The Life and Work of Leo XIII," 20.

3. Owen Chadwick, *A History of the Popes 1830–1914* (Oxford: Clarendon Press, 1998), 275–76.

4. Eamon Duffy, *Saints and Sinners: A History of the Popes,* 2nd ed. (New Haven/London: Yale University Press, 2001), 306.

5. Alec R. Vidler, *20th Century Defenders of the Faith* (London: SCM Press, 1965), 34.

6. Chadwick, *History of the Popes,* 281.

7. Duffy, *Saints and Sinners,* 317.

8. Chadwick, *History of the Popes,* 284.

9. Ibid., 299.

10. Duffy, *Saints and Sinners,* 311.

11. Sheridan Gilley, "Pope Leo's Legacy," *The Tablet* (December 13, 2003): 10.

12. Owen Chadwick, *A History of Christianity* (London: Weidenfeld and Nicholson, 1995), 248.

13. Duffy, *Saints and Sinners,* 312.

14. Ibid., 313.

15. Chadwick, *History of the Popes 1830–1914,* 281.

16. James Collins, "Leo XIII and the Philosophical Approach to Modernity," in *Leo XIII and the Modern World,* ed. Gargan, 200.

17. Duffy, *Saints and Sinners,* 314.

18. "Note on the Import of the Doctrinal Decrees Concerning the Thought and Works of the Priest Antonio Rosmini-Serbati," n. 6, Vatican City, July 1, 2001, noted from *New Catholic Encyclopedia,* 2nd ed. (Detroit: Thomson/Gale in association with The Catholic University of America, 2003), 12:384.

19. Cited from Schmandt, "Life and Work of Leo XIII," 39. There is a useful summary of the encyclical in *The New Jerome Biblical Commentary,* ed. Raymond E. Brown, SS, Joseph A. Fitzmyer, SJ, and Roland E. Murphy, OCarm (Englewood Cliffs, NJ: Prentice Hall, 1990), 1167–68.

20. Gustave Weigel, SJ, "Leo XIII and Contemporary Theology," in *Leo XIII and the Modern World,* ed. Gargan, 217.

21. See John M. T. Barton, "The Dominican School in Jerusalem and Old Testament Studies," in *Lagrange and Biblical Renewal,* ed. Richard T. Murphy, OP (Chicago: Priory Press, 1966), 5–46, esp. 21–22.

22. Owen Chadwick, *Catholicism and History: The Opening of the Vatican Archives* (Cambridge: Cambridge University Press, 1978), 92.

23. Cited from Schmandt, "Life and Work of Leo XIII," 39.

24. See David J. O'Brien, "Americanism," in *The Encyclopedia of American Catholic History,* ed. Michael Glazier and Thomas Shelley (Collegeville, MN: Liturgical Press, 1997), 97–99.

25. Margaret M. Reher, "Leo XIII and Americanism," *Theological Studies* 34 (1973): 681.

26. The entire text of the letter is printed at the end of David O'Brien's article, "Americanism" (n. 24 above). Here the citation is from p. 103.

27. Avery Dulles, SJ, reaches the same conclusion (*A History of Apologetics* [New York: Corpus Books, 1971], 190–91).

28. Thus Duffy, *Saints and Sinners,* 316; see also Reher, "Leo XIII and Americanism," 689.

29. Cited from Schmandt, "Life and Work of Leo XIII," 46.

30. Eric McDermott, SJ, "Leo XIII and England," in *Leo XIII and the Modern World,* ed. Gargan, 145.

31. From the English text in *Anglican Orders: Essays on the Centenary of Apostolicae Curae 1896-1996,* ed. R. W. Franklin (Harrisburg, PA: Morehouse, 1996), 136.

32. Philippe Levillain, "Leo XIII," in *The Papacy: An Encyclopedia,* ed. Philippe Levillain (New York/London: Routledge, 2002), 2:935.

8
THE MODERNIST CRISIS

Perhaps the most widely shared idea among the Modernists was the conviction that scholastic theology was inadequate to interpret Christianity in the modern age. Because it was so entrenched many of them, especially the priests, reacted violently against it, adopting current philosophical speculations, or symbolist interpretations of doctrine, or drifting into skepticism.
—Meriol Trevor[1]

As one reads this introductory quotation from Meriol Trevor, one is struck by its very contemporary ring. Scholastic theology, despite its continually rediscovered richness of insight, is inadequate to interpret Christianity for our times. Thinking *with* Aquinas is altogether different from thinking *as* Aquinas. The reaction against scholastic theology, including Thomistic theology, after Vatican II is very similar to the reaction of the modernists at the beginning of the twentieth century. In addition, Vatican II has been followed by some of the problematic directions noted by Trevor—adopting current philosophical speculations with an inadequate appreciation of past philosophical achievement, symbolist interpretations of Christian doctrine, and even some forms of skepticism. Our own times and issues at the beginning of the twenty-first century are remarkably close to the modernist times at the beginning of the twentieth century. An analysis of modernism should aid our contemporary self-understanding.

An enormous amount of excellent research has been done on modernism in the last thirty years or so. One of the foremost commentators on modernism of the last generation, Roger

Aubert, offers a useful starting point for our thinking: "The term 'modernism' was in use since the sixteenth century to characterize the tendency to esteem the modern age more highly than antiquity."[2] In this precise sense of the word, *modernism* is a constant feature of the church at all times, and thus includes the church of our times. It points to the attempt better to enable the mission of the church through recourse to the new insights and ideas and methodologies that the "modern" generation offers. It is the church constantly trying to renew and to reform itself, as it were, but with the omnipresent human tendency to downgrade the past, thinking that all human wisdom is of very recent vintage.

While aware of crude generalization, and most especially in the understanding of the modernism of the late nineteenth and early twentieth centuries, one might say that the modernists in general were convinced that theology had been much too intellectualist and abstract, and they desired to reconcile the church with the modern world by developing theologies that were closer knit to life and action, more organic, more experientially based. The nineteenth century had witnessed more experientially based ways of doing theology—one thinks especially of the work of Friedrich Schleiermacher—and evolution, or perhaps developmentalism, was axiomatic in philosophic thought, with Darwin and Newman coming to mind. Before looking at the classical modernists, we ought first to consider briefly some of the earlier nineteenth-century precursors.

Before Modernism

Although modernism was a late-nineteenth-century and early-twentieth-century phenomenon, it had precursors in the earlier part of the nineteenth century in scholars who desired the church to adapt to at least some aspects of modernity.

Félicité de Lamennais (1782–1854)

This French ultramontane philosopher was a pioneer of Catholic liberalism. Although as a young man Lamennais was attracted to the rationalism characteristic of the French Revolution, he was won back to the faith by his older brother, Jean Marie de Lamennais, who was a devout priest. Lamennais' historical studies led him to the conviction that union between church and state does not aid the church. He advocated a Catholic revival, but with the church entirely free of state influence and control. "God and Liberty" became his motto. He equally advocated for the state the liberalism that was consequent upon the French Revolution. He thought that the ideals and convictions of the revolution could be Catholicized.

> He argued that the people—not the aristocracy, or the episcopacy, or the bourgeoisie, but the common people, the peasants and artisans, the class which came to be called the proletariat…was emerging for the first time in history and would control the future.[3]

For him Christianity was ineluctably *social.*

At the same time, he came to see the way forward in the development of ultramontanism—a natural alliance between pope and people—and so in 1830 Lamennais and his associates started the paper *L'Avenir,* the first Catholic daily paper, a decidedly liberal publication, publishing articles and editorials advocating separation of church and state and democratic government.[4] The pope should be the mainstay and support of people everywhere in their pursuit of freedom and justice, and not the traditional ally of princes and power. This did not sit well with the Gallican episcopate in France, who did not wish for any further extension of papal powers into the French national church. Nor did it find support in the various courts of Europe. Lamennais tried to have Pope Gregory XVI endorse his principles, but to no avail. While he was in Rome with his associates seeking papal approval for his ideas, both politicians and bishops were bombarding Pope Gregory XVI with complaints about his dangerous liberalism. His positions earned condemnation by Rome in the encyclical *Mirari Vos* (1832) and were described as "absurd," "perverse," "ludicrous" and "execrable." There was a certain naiveté in Lamennais' hope that revolutionary ideas like democracy and tolerance would be espoused by the church in the wake of 1789. Equally, however, as Meriol Trevor points out, "How surprised Pope Gregory XVI would have been by the declaration on Religious Liberty of the Second Vatican Council!"[5] Eventually in 1834, both frustrated and utterly demoralized, Lamennais published his book *Paroles d'un croyant* and abandoned the priesthood. Probably more than anyone else, Lamennais made ultramontanism popular in France, even paving the way for its more extreme versions, and contributed to the weakening of Gallicanism. He died in 1854, aged seventy-two, unreconciled with the church.

Ignaz von Döllinger (1799–1890)

Professor of church history at the University of Munich, Döllinger promoted in and for the church high standards of critical historical scholarship. He had an organic and developmental view of history, key expressions being "organic growth" and "consistent development." He interpreted Protestantism as a fundamental break with the organic and developing tradition of Christianity. He became increasingly suspicious of the centralization of papal authority and governance, favoring a more nationally based church. He experienced the growing interest in scholastic theology as inimical to his brand of historical scholarship. He refused to accept the papal position as outlined in *Pastor Aeternus* of Vatican I and was excommunicated. He had contact with those who formed the Old Catholics after Vatican I, but did not himself join their schismatic movement.[6] As a priest, Döllinger could no longer celebrate Mass, but he continued to attend the celebration. After experiencing a stroke in 1890, Döllinger received the sacrament of extreme unction [anointing of the sick] from Johann Friedrich, another priest-church historian who had joined the Old Catholics. Dom Cuthbert Butler, OSB, notes carefully: "Every priest, even excommunicate, as Friedrich was, has faculties *in articulo mortis* [in danger of death]."[7]

Lord Acton (1834–1902)

In England, Lord Acton and the circle around him set out to renew Catholic literary, historical, and scientific culture. An English aristocrat, John Emerich Dalberg Acton spent one year at St. Nicholas, a preparatory school near Paris under Felix Dupanloup (later to be bishop of Orleans and to play, as we have seen, a significant role at Vatican I); four years at St. Mary's College, Oscott, in the English Midlands, at that time under the direction of Nicholas Wiseman (later to become cardinal-archbishop of Westminster); then he continued his studies under a private tutor in Edinburgh for one year. Finally, in 1850, Acton became the pupil of Ignaz von Döllinger, a church historian, with whom he formed a deep and lasting relationship.

> Döllinger impressed upon Acton the primacy of history in the study of theology. No longer could a serious Catholic scholar be content with a systematic theology derived from medieval schoolmen notoriously ignorant of history. To think seriously about society was to think historically, and in the world of history the law of development was the only constant.[8]

Acton, influenced and shaped by Döllinger, became a very considerable historian, ultimately appointed Regius Professor of Modern History at Cambridge in 1894, a post he held until his death in 1902.

His historical interests and background made him suspicious of Pio Nono's *Syllabus of Errors* and also of the ultramontanism leading up to Vatican I in 1869–1870. In Acton's judgment papal absolutism, personified in Pius, was the great evil from which the church had to be rescued if it was adequately to lead people to Christ. This, needless to say, made him enormously suspect in ultramontane quarters, especially when he was in Rome reporting on the First Vatican Council. Nonetheless, his close friendship with Döllinger did not lead him, as it did his teacher, to leave the church after the definition of papal infallibility. The church was much too important in his own life for that to happen to Acton, who fervently believed that writing faithful history could never "involve contradiction with the teaching or authority of the Church whose communion is dearer to me than life."[9] He taught his son in 1890, "A Church without a pope is not the Church of Christ."[10]

These anticipations of modernism got nowhere. Both Lamennais and Döllinger were to leave the church and died excommunicate, and Acton got nowhere as a defender of a modern Catholicism. In the words of the English historian of modernism Alec Vidler, "The papacy would have none of them."[11]

Four Modernists: Loisy, Tyrrell, Laberthonnière, Le Roy

The distinctive feature of Catholic Modernism lies in the concomitant claim of the right, nonetheless, to retain the entire fabric of the traditional and devotional practice of Latin Christendom—reinterpreted, however, as an apparatus of beautiful and psychologically effective symbolism, and justified on the basis of a subjectivist philosophy which introduced a cleavage between devotional value on the one hand and intellectual or factual truth on the other.[12]

This description of modernism by Aidan Nichols, OP, could be debated in various ways, but it throws into high relief one perceived, significant aspect of modernism, that is, that it seemed to reduce the objective truth of the faith to subjective, symbolic interpretation. The dogmatic truths of the Christian faith seem to become, in the hands of modernism, symbolic expressions of human experience. Behind this phenomenon lie the disciplines of history suggesting powerfully the development of doctrine over time and circumstances. History becomes overwhelming to the point of reducing truth to what seems appropriate here and now. A certain historical relativism has emerged. We might also add to this reductionistic approach to Christian doctrine an excessive emphasis on divine immanence and perhaps a complete liberation of scientific research from contact with faith or doctrine.

Alfred Loisy (1857–1940)

Alfred Loisy, a farmer's son, went on to study for the priesthood, and, as his intellectual gifts were recognized, he became a professor of biblical and oriental studies at the Institut Catholique in Paris. Though he had told his good friend, Monsignor Eudoxe-Irénée-Edouard, bishop of Albi, that he wished to exercise a priestly and pastoral role in the church and not an academic career, it is the latter that became his lot.[13] He was a pupil of the great historian Louis Duchesne. He also attended the lectures of Ernest Renan, the author of the famous *Life of Jesus,* and it is probably from Renan that he developed his interest in biblical criticism. Loisy was concerned not simply to develop an academic career in his theological specialties, but also to help the church respond to the pastoral and intellectual needs of the time. Initially, in 1890, his appointment at the Institut Catholique was as professor of holy scripture, his doctoral thesis being on the history of the Old Testament canon. After difficulties connected with his scripture studies, the rector, Monsignor D'Hulst, appointed Loisy to the teaching of Hebrew and Oriental languages, deemed safer than the dangerous terrain of scripture.

Loisy's controversial book *The Gospel and the Church* was published in 1902. In one respect, this book was an answer to the Berlin historian and theologian Adolf von Harnack's book *What Is Christianity?* Essentially, Harnack reduced Christianity to two fundamental ideas, the fatherhood of God and the brotherhood of humans. Everything else is unessential. Harnack believed that the hellenization of Christianity, both during and especially after the first century of the church, was a corruption of this simple gospel. Not for Loisy. In *The Gospel and the Church* Loisy responds to Harnack's liberal Protestantism, but he also sets out to show that the essence of the gospel is perpetuated in the Catholic Church. Against Harnack, Loisy set forth the notion that the historical Jesus was no Harnackian liberal teacher, but a Jew who believed in an imminent end to the world. Further, in response to Harnack's attempt to strip away all these hellenized accretions to modern Christianity and return to the absolute fundamentals of the religion, Loisy asks: "Why not find the essence of Christianity in the fullness and totality of its life, which shows movement and vitality just because it is life?"[14] The entire historical continuum of the Christian tradition revealed what Christianity was. The evolution of the tradition responded to the different cultural and spiritual needs of life at different stages.

Thus far Loisy's project seems fine; however, there was more to Loisy's book than that. Loisy was convinced of the necessity of ongoing approaches in history to dogma and doctrine in the life of the church. No dogma or doctrine was an expression of absolute truth, but rather was an imperfect symbol, forged out of human experience but having its origin in Christian life and action. Loisy's principles are best summarized in his own words. He presented his project as:

> Firstly, as an outline and historical explanation of the development of Christianity and then as a general

philosophy of religion and an effort to interpret the dogmas, the official creeds and the definitions of the Councils, the purpose of which is to reconcile them with the realities of history and the mentality of our contemporaries, by sacrificing the letter to the spirit.[15]

There was a very real relativizing of the doctrinal tradition of the church in Loisy's theology. The book engendered a fear: Where would this relativizing stop? Would all and every doctrine become nothing more than a symbolic expression of developing human experience? Was nothing safe, as it were?

When Loisy wrote *The Gospel and the Church,* it seems that he no longer believed in traditional christological doctrine, though he still believed in the living God. In fact, this notion of the mystery of the transcendent God never left him. Vidler comments: "Perhaps Loisy's agnosticism had more reverence in it, and even more faith, than the confident dogmatism of those who condemned him."[16] Vidler may be right, but there is also in Loisy a certain bitterness toward authority, a bitterness that never benefits anyone. His approach to dogma, doctrine, and truth, and his inadequate Christology were bound to get him into difficulties. The final break with the church for Loisy took place in 1908. In that year he was publicly excommunicated— an act described by Trevor as "an unusual severity."[17] The following year he was elected to a chair at the Collège de France.

What of Loisy's own, personal relationship with Christianity, with Christian faith? Did that come to an end with his condemnation and exit from the church? It is notoriously difficult to grasp the interiority of another. We must be content with whatever limited facts may be available, and with particular points of view based on immediate experience. Alec Vidler, for example, a historian of modernism, who visited Loisy a number of times in the 1930s, long after his excommunication, describes him in these terms: "I can only say for my part that I do not doubt the sincerity of his faith and of his allegiance to the Church up to the time when the Church demanded a retraction of his modernist convictions."[18] Vidler saw Loisy as a faithful and sincere Christian, at least up to the moment of his excommunication. From two of Loisy's autobiographical writings, *Choses Passées* and *Mémoires,* it seems that he experienced a crisis of faith before 1886. This probably had to do with his idea of the failure of scholastic orthodoxy, which emerged as his biblical studies began to develop. Vidler was not close to Loisy, but Maude Petre was, and she related to Vidler the following memory:

> Miss Petre told me that she had some years before (1941) attended a conference at Pontigny at which Loisy also was present. He could not go into the Abbey church for the solemn mass on Sunday since he was *vitandus,* but he was discovered outside with tears in his eyes.[19]

Vidler makes the interesting distinction that, though Loisy could no longer operate liturgically as a priest after his excommunication, he continued to be a priest *religiously.* By this Vidler meant that he continued to show concern with the religious aspect of human nature, and even to some extent, with pastoral ministry. The epitaph that he drew up for himself contains the following words: "Alfred Loisy, a priest retired from the ministry...Professor at the Collège de France, kept your will in his vows *(tuam in votis tenuit voluntatem).*" Obviously, Loisy continued to think of himself as a priest in some basic sense of that word.

Particularly difficult for Loisy was an experience he had in 1904. He had written a letter to Pope Pius X in which he had made an active submission to the condemnation of his books. The letter began: "Most Holy Father, I well know your Holiness' goodness of heart and it is to your heart that I now address myself." On March 12 that year, Cardinal François-Marie-Benjamin Richard of Paris gave him the papal reply in which he read these words: "I have received a letter from the

Rev. Abbé Loisy, in which he appeals to my heart, but this letter was not written from the heart." In Loisy's book, *Choses Passées,* he described the effect of the letter:

> Something gave way within me when I heard the opening words. The head of this church to which I had given my life, for which I had worked so hard for thirty years past, which I had loved and could not help loving still, outside of which I had no hopes nor ambitions, could find nothing else to say, when I had responded to absurd demands by a supreme sacrifice, than the harsh words: "that letter addressed to my heart was not written from the heart." All the same, it was written from the heart. Pressed into it was the last drop of feeling left in my Catholic soul.[20]

George Tyrrell (1861–1909)

George Tyrrell was an Irishman, a convert to Catholicism from Anglicanism, who became a priest member of the Society of Jesus. His brother, Willie, ten years his senior, won prizes and scholarships at Trinity College, Dublin. George went to Rathmines School in Dublin, where the principal, Dr. C. W. Benson, could count eighty-five clergymen, including two bishops, from his pupils. In 1879, George Tyrrell was received into the Catholic Church by Fr. Albany Christie, SJ, of Farm St., and then he joined the Society of Jesus. He had been well trained in scholasticism, with a particular enthusiasm for St. Thomas himself. He did his theological studies at St. Beuno's in Wales, where Gerard Manley Hopkins had been a student, and was ordained a priest in 1891. After some initial teaching, he was given over to preaching, retreats, instructing converts, and writing for the Jesuit periodical *The Month.* Eventually he was dismissed from the Society in 1906, though not from the priesthood.

It was Friedrich von Hügel who opened his eyes to the limitations of the scholastic way of thinking and to the new ways of studying the Bible and Christian history. Alec Vidler believes that Tyrrell was at his best when writing about the spiritual life, and Aidan Nichols calls him a "spiritual writer of genius."[21] He defines a modernist as "a churchman of any sort who believes in the possibility of a synthesis between the essential truth of his religion and the essential truth of modernity."[22] At least in intention if nothing else, we may see in this clear statement that modernists were not out to assail the church, but to contribute to its mission through renewal and reform.

For Tyrrell, throughout his written work, Christ did not present himself primarily as a teacher of orthodoxy. Theology and dogma were but feeble human efforts to grasp in intellectual terms the divine force and energy at work in humankind, a position very close to Loisy. *Christianity at the Crossroads* was published in 1909. He believed that Catholicism held more promise than other faiths of becoming a universal religion:

> [It] is more nearly a microcosm of the world of religions than any other known form; where we find nearly every form of religious expression, from the lowest to the highest, pressed together and straining towards unification and coherence; where the ideal of universal and perpetual validity has ever been an explicit aim; where, moreover, this ideal is clothed in a form that cannot possibly endure the test of history and science and must undergo some transformation.[23]

The test of the fruitfulness of a belief, for Tyrrell, is to be found not only in its moral implications, as with the pragmatism of Laberthonnière and Le Roy, but also in its devotional and spiritual consequences: "Beliefs that have been found by continuous and invariable experience to foster and promote the spiritual life of the soul must so far be in accord with the nature and the laws of that will-world with which it is the aim of religion to bring us into harmony."[24]

Meriol Trevor is entirely accurate when she describes Tyrrell in these words:

> He did not really advance the cause of reform. First because his expressions of protest were too extreme, putting off the ordinary Catholic; secondly because he too distorted the facts. Too often he accepted the identification of the Church with the clerical organization, even while he attacked it.[25]

In March 1909, Tyrrell suffered an attack of gastric influenza, though the truer picture was that he was in the last stages of Bright's disease. Tyrrell died on July 9, 1909, reconciled to the church, in Maude Petre's house in Storrington. This was in the Diocese of Southwark, south of the Thames. Because Tyrrell had not retracted his modernist errors on his deathbed, Bishop Peter Amigo refused to permit a Catholic burial for him.[26] To say the least, even given the antimodernist temper of the times, this seems pusillanimous. Tyrrell was buried in a corner of the Anglican parish cemetery of Storrington. That same year, 1909, Loisy took his chair at the Collège de France.

Lucien Laberthonnière (1860–1932)

Laberthonnière was a priest of the Congregation of the Oratory. Even as a young seminarian, he found himself increasingly dissatisfied with what Alec Vidler calls "the confidence and complacency of the official scholastic theology."[27] He became a professor of philosophy at the Oratorian Collège de Juilly in 1887 and remained in that position until 1903, when the French government moved against religious congregations. He thought of himself specifically as a Christian philosopher and so spoke about a "metaphysic of charity" and sometimes of "moral dogmatism." This latter phrase points to an understanding of dogma more as a practical guide for Christian living than as divinely guaranteed conceptual inroads to the divine mystery. Dogmas show "what we are and what we ought to be and how we can become what we ought to be."[28] Moral dogmatism is an approach to Christian dogma that wrings out the practical, moral, and social meaning of dogma as a support and direction for living the Christian life, representing a very practical and very personalist view of religion. If truth is to be had, it must be had *from* living and *for* living. If the objection is made that this approach to religious truth appears to push out the divine and to espouse a purely natural approach, Laberthonnière would reply that the natural is already penetrated by the divine. In a real sense, there is no such thing as the purely natural, but rather the natural is "the prolongation of the divine life into the life of man."[29]

Laberthonnière was hostile to Thomism. He saw Thomism as an instance of Greek idealism, abstract and arid and lacking vitality, in contrast to Christian realism, which was dynamic, personal, and social. He once wrote to von Hügel who had praised Aquinas in the preface to one of his books:

> To me—I say it to you in all simplicity—he appears to stand doctrinally for a radical anti-Christianity. In place of the Gospel's God of love he put an egocentric God…for him the Church consists essentially in the ecclesiastical organization regarded as a *domination* that is to be exercised under the direction and to the advantage of theologians….[30]

Really, this is a travesty of Aquinas, understandable perhaps as a reaction to an ecclesiastically imposed scholasticism, but a travesty nonetheless. There can be little doubt that Laberthonnière's "persistent and violent anti-Thomism" (in Vidler's description) led to his being viewed with suspicion by Rome.

His major philosophical books, *Essays on Religious Philosophy* and *Christian Realism and Greek Idealism* were placed on the Index of Prohibited Books in 1906, as were other works by him in 1913, and he was forbidden to publish. In both publications he saw Thomism as a version of "Greek idealism"—that is abstract, not having anything to do with the vital flow of life. The test of any given philosophy, as Laberthonnière understood it, is whether it can be illuminating and helpful when brought to bear on the issues and problems of life. Christian realism was much more successful in relating to life than any form of Greek idealism, including Aristotelianism and Thomism.

Laberthonnière was equally uncompromising in his negative reaction to papal authority. Rightly, he viewed the role of authority as one of service, not domination (Mark 10:45), but he saw no exercise of contemporary authority as being marked by service. Although Laberthonnière was a rebel against authority, Vidler maintains that "[h]e stood for resistance, but not for revolt."[31] Reform had to come from *within* the community of faith and, above all else, Laberthonnière wanted reform. Concerning the encyclical *Pascendi,* he wrote: "Silent, persevering, mortified work will do more than anything else."[32]

Edouard Le Roy (1870–1954)

"LeRoy, it is true, is not so well known as his fellow Modernists Alfred Loisy and George Tyrrell, but this Gallic logician…penetrates to the heart of the Modernists' difficulties with traditional Catholicism."[33] Joseph Fitzer in this comment is pointing to Le Roy's influential essay, "What Is a Dogma?" but, before we turn to this, we should say something about the man.

Edouard Le Roy was a layman, a philosopher, a student of Henri Bergson, and a very devout Catholic. He developed his teacher's evolutionary philosophy toward "a Christian 'psychistic' idealism," the notion that all reality has at least the potential for psychic life. The more concentrated an organism is in terms of growing complexity, the more "psychic" it is. In humankind, evolution continues on the plane of spirit, ever subject to the divine transcendent-creative action. If this sounds somewhat like Teilhard, there is an obvious reason. Le Roy was very friendly with Pierre Teilhard de Chardin, SJ. Vidler writes of their friendship: "There was an obvious concordance and concurrence in their ideas about the meaning of history and the cosmos."[34] At Le Roy's death in 1954, Teilhard wrote:

> There are few men whom I have so deeply admired and loved as I did him. So serene, so completely human—and so deeply Christian....I owed him a very great debt. It was not exactly that I owed any particular idea to him, but that, particularly between 1920 and 1930, he gave me confidence, enlarged my mind (and my feeling of loyalty to the Church), and served (at the Collège de France) as a spokesman for my ideas, then taking shape on "hominization" and the "noosphere."[35]

Le Roy's association with modernism stems from his treatment of dogma in an article of 1905, "What Is a Dogma?" and a book of 1907, *Dogma and Criticism,* which was put on the Index of Prohibited Books. Although Le Roy submitted formally to the judgment of the church, he did not actually abandon his ideas. Dogma for him does not so much convey positive knowledge as it guards against false ideas. Dogma has a negative sense, but it also has a practical purpose. It is a rule of practical conduct. Thus, for example, to affirm that God is personal tells us less something positive about God, and more that personal relations are to be thought of as ultimately valuable. Again, the resurrection of Christ is less an affirmation of a past event than a personal commitment to live as a contemporary of Christ.

Even after his books were placed on the Index, Le Roy never broke with the church. Philosophically, he valued the church very highly as the premier institution in the West for encouraging religious attitudes and action. More pragmatically, he recognized that any realistic attempt to renew or reform the church must come from within. As Vidler puts it: "He realized that identification with the Church involved being apparently identified with elements in it which one deplored, but that was not a sufficient reason for breaking away: on the contrary, reform was possible only from within."[36]

Le Roy's book *Dogma and Criticism* ends with these words:

> To my opponents whom I wish to regard as my friends, I confidently address…this appeal before God: let us help one another to grow in the truth and let us strive for unity rather than to triumph over one another. We profess the same faith, we share in the same life, we are committed to the same obedience, we have communion in the same prayer, we have at heart the same desire and the same love.

The understanding of dogma in Laberthonnière and Le Roy is very close. Both emphasized the pragmatic meaning of dogma. Although one can hardly quarrel with that—the Christian life necessarily has to do with *how to live*—dogma is understood to do more. It is the least inadequate language for speaking of God and things divine. All language about God is problematic to some degree. Language, including dogmatic language, is, in Herbert McCabe, OP's wonderful term "second hand clothes" for God. None of it fits perfectly. But a Catholic approach also recognizes accuracy about God in dogmatic language, even if accuracy may not be construed as intellectual exactitude. This seems to be the dimension missing from Laberthonnière and Le Roy. Unlike Loisy and some others, Laberthonnière and Le Roy recognized the need to work for ecclesial reform from within.

The Church's Response

The church's response to modernism in terms of Pope Pius X will be examined in a later chapter. It would be foolish to claim that there was no such thing as "modernism," but it is not easy to say what it was. It was not a coordinated group or party within the church with a particular set of consistent ideas to which those in the group assented. Rather, it was a group within the church who desired to adapt the church and its teachings to the modern world, especially the modern world of philosophical and theological scholarship. It is, however, undoubtedly true that the philosophical and theological ideas of the modernists were often misrepresented by those who found them alienating or even threatening. Nonetheless, had the thought of those deemed modernists been allowed to develop and to be challenged in a scholarly fashion, it is possible that the so-called modernist crisis may not have been the *debacle* it turned out to be. If the crudities of positions taken had been refined in the fires of scholarly, analytic exchange, extreme judgments might have been avoided.

Aidan Nichols writes: "The truly regrettable aspect of the reaction…was the semi-official connivance at the creation of a veritable Counter-Modernist espionage ring by Mgr. Umberto Benigni (1862–1934)…."[37] Benigni was only able to do this with the support of Pius X, and it is to this pope's complex character and background that we must turn for details of the reaction to modernism.

Bibliography

Trevor, Meriol. *Prophets and Guardians: Renewal and Tradition in the Church.* London/Sydney/Toronto: Hollis and Carter, 1969.

Vidler, Alec R. *20th Century Defenders of the Faith.* London: SCM Press, 1965.

———. *A Variety of Catholic Modernists.* Cambridge: Cambridge University Press, 1970.

Notes

1. Meriol Trevor, *Prophets and Guardians: Renewal and Tradition in the Church* (London/Sydney/Toronto: Hollis and Carter, 1969), 86.

2. Roger Aubert, "Modernism," in *Sacramentum Mundi,* ed. Karl Rahner, SJ, et al. (New York: Herder and Herder, 1969), 4:99.

3. E. E. Y. Hales, *The Catholic Church in the Modern World* (Garden City, NY: Hanover House, 1958), 89.

4. Trevor *(Prophets and Guardians,* 146) suggests that there is a similarity between Lamennais' *L'Avenir* and the Oxford Movement's *Tracts for the Times,* begun in 1833. Both recognized the importance of "the cheap printed word as a means of rapid communication of ideas."

5. Trevor, *Prophets and Guardians,* 150.

6. See Pontien Pulman, OFM, "Historical Background of Old Catholicism," in *Historical Problems of Church Renewal,* ed. Roger Aubert and Anton Weiler (Glen Rock, NJ: Paulist Press, 1965), 158–67.

7. Cuthbert Butler, OSB., *The Vatican Council* (London/New York: Longmans Green, 1930), 2:190.

8. Hugh A. Macdougall, *Lord Acton on Papal Power* (London: Sheed and Ward, 1973), 3. A fine, brief appreciation of Acton as a historian may be found in Owen Chadwick, *Professor Lord Acton* (Grand Rapids: Acton Institute, 1995).

9. Macdougall, *Lord Acton on Papal Power,* 17.

10. Reported in H. A. Macdougall, "Acton, John Emerich Edward Dalberg," *New Catholic Encyclopedia,* 2nd ed. (Detroit: Thomson/Gale in association with The Catholic University of America, 2003), 1:85.

11. Alec R. Vidler, *20th Century Defenders of the Faith* (London: SCM Press, 1965), 33.

12. Aidan Nichols, OP, *Catholic Thought since the Enlightenment: A Survey* (Leominster, UK: Gracewing, 1998), 83-84.

13. Alec R. Vidler, *A Variety of Catholic Modernists* (Cambridge: Cambridge University Press, 1970), 30.

14. Alfred Loisy, *The Gospel and the Church* (New York: Charles Scribner's Sons, 1912), 16.

15. From an essay by Loisy of 1906, cited in Nichols, *Catholic Thought since the Enlightenment,* 85.

16. Vidler, *Variety of Catholic Modernists,* 53.

17. Trevor, *Prophets and Guardians,* 66.

18. Vidler, *20th Century Defenders of the Faith,* 46.

19. Vidler, *Variety of Catholic Modernists,* 11.

20. Cited in Vidler, *Variety of Catholic Modernists,* 47.

21. Vidler, *20th Century Defenders of the Faith,* 47; Nichols, *Catholic Thought since the Enlightenment,* 86.

22. George Tyrrell, *Christianity at the Crossroads* (London/ New York: Longmans Green, 1909), 5.

23. Ibid., 167.

24. George Tyrrell, *Lex Orandi* (London/New York: Longmans, 1903), 57.

25. Trevor, *Prophets and Guardians,* 72.

26. For details, see Clyde F. Crews, *English Catholic Modernism: Maude Petre's Way of Faith* (Notre Dame, IN: University of Notre Dame Press, 1984), 54–56.

27. Vidler, *Variety of Catholic Modernists,* 82.

28. Lucien Laberthonnière, *Theory of Education* (1935), 77, cited in Vidler, *Variety of Catholic Modernists,* 83.

29. See John Macquarrie, *Twentieth Century Religious Thought* (London: SCM Press, 1963), 183–84.

30. Cited in Vidler, *Variety of Catholic Modernists,* 85–86.

31. Vidler, *Variety of Catholic Modernists,* 87.

32. Ibid.

33. Joseph Fitzer, *Romance and the Rock: Nineteenth Century Catholics on Reason and Faith* (Minneapolis: Augsburg Press, 1989), 9.

34. Vidler, *Variety of Catholic Modernists,* 93.

35. Claude Cuenot, *Teilhard de Chardin: A Biographical Study* (Baltimore: Helicon Press, 1961), 58.

36. Vidler, *Variety of Catholic Modernists,* 92.

37. Nichols, *Catholic Thought since the Enlightenment,* 88.

BARON FRIEDRICH VON HÜGEL (1852–1925)

For von Hügel learning was a religious passion.
—Ellen M. Leonard[1]

Von Hügel, maintains Alec Vidler, was "the chief engineer of the modernist movement," that is to say, he stimulated and encouraged potential modernists, kept them in touch with one another's work, all in an effort to reform and renew Catholicism.[2] Von Hügel devotees may not especially like this judgment, but it does seem to have been the case, though with a qualification we shall enter later. Despite his progressivist views on scripture and theology, von Hügel, like Le Roy, was very devout in his practice of Catholicism. "His style of piety at once reflected and sustained his unshakeable attachment to the Church—his daily visit to the Blessed Sacrament, his recitation of the Rosary, etc...."[3]

Life

Friedrich von Hügel was the son of a Scottish mother, Elizabeth Farquharson, a convert to Catholicism from Presbyterianism, and an Austrian diplomat, Carl Alexander Anselm von Hügel, who was a baron of the Holy Roman Empire. Friedrich's early life was spent in Tuscany and Belgium. In 1867 the family settled in England. He was educated privately by a variety of tutors. His culture was cosmopolitan, and his religious affinities were ecumenical. His erudition embraced philosophy, theology, history, biblical criticism, and geology. He combined this massive, largely self-taught scholarship—Nicholas Lash calls him an "immensely learned amateur"[4]—with a deep spiritual life and devotion to the Catholic Church. Living in London, von Hügel spent a great deal of his time studying in the British Museum reading room.

What von Hügel referred to as his "first conversion" began when he witnessed a particular incident in the cathedral of Mainz. He watched from behind a pillar while a distraught young woman prayed in front of the high altar. Apparently, her baby had just died. She came away from the altar comforted.[5] This had a profound affect on him. In the words of Meriol Trevor, "He had watched an encounter with God and felt that his doubts on the efficacy of prayer were ended."[6] In 1870, the year of the First Vatican Council, von Hügel's turning to prayer, as it were, was aided by a Dutch Dominican in Vienna, Fr. Raymond Hocking.

In 1873, von Hügel married Lady Mary Herbert, a convert to Catholicism. John Henry Newman wrote to Lady Mary, promising to celebrate Mass for her and Friedrich on their wedding day, November 27. In the ensuing years, they had three daughters: Gertrud, Hildegard, and Thekla. Friedrich was devoted to his children in every respect, and not least in their education. Though Lady Mary had a rather simple and uncomplicated Christian faith and did not share her husband's *penchant* for theological and philosophical analysis, she entertained with Friedrich a constant stream of visitors and scholars in their home in London. Michael de la Bedoyere writes that von Hügel had an "intimate acquaintance with all the leading religious figures in Britain, France, Italy, and Germany, to all of whom he could speak and write in their own tongue."[7]

During a visit to France in 1884, von Hügel was introduced to the Abbé Henri Huvelin. From this French spiritual guide von Hügel found a sense of direction through his multiple intellectual pursuits. Huvelin was attached to a large Parisian parish and was well established as a gifted spiritual director. It was through Huvelin's ministrations that Charles de Foucauld was converted, finally going as a hermit to the Sahara and his death. "It was this powerful influence from a true mystic which later helped the Baron to stay within the Church when many of his friends were leaving it."[8]

This great theological autodidact received an honorary degree from the University of St. Andrews, Scotland, in 1914, his very first academic honor. His Scottish roots were further strengthened when the University of Edinburgh invited him to give the prestigious Gifford Lectures in the session 1924–1926 and proposed to confer on him the degree of Doctor of Divinity. Ill health prevented him from delivering the Giffords, but the lectures were published posthumously as *The Reality of God.*[9] He was buried in the cemetery at Downside Abbey.

Modernism

Scholars evaluate von Hügel's role in the modernist movement quite differently. Meriol Trevor writes: "He made himself a kind of international communications officer, introducing people from different countries to each other and sending books and letters across the frontiers."[10] This is certainly true. When von Hügel came across a persuasive position in a new book or learned article, he introduced it to those who he considered would be particularly open. He also introduced new ideas in theology to those who he thought should be open. It is true that he held positions not especially favored by the church, not least in the area of scripture. He was in touch with Alfred Loisy for years. Nor could he be considered an ultramontane in his ecclesiology.

Von Hügel had a profound influence on others, particularly George Tyrrell, SJ. Thus, during the decades of the modernist movement from 1890 to 1910, von Hügel found himself deeply troubled, especially when his friend George Tyrrell fell afoul of the church. Undoubtedly he must have been concerned about his role in the *debacle*. He himself did not waiver in his own ecclesial faith and belonging. It may be that there was in von Hügel a certain naiveté when it came to the study of theology and the Vatican. He was guilty of naiveté very possibly, but never of any malice. His immense delight in theological and philosophical learning left him in some degree innocent of ecclesiastical attitudes and politics. Von Hügel's own personal piety and devotion, his mystical dimension, kept him within the church. Meriol Trevor puts it like this: "Anchored as he was in a spiritual life fed by eucharistic devotion and by his love of historical actuality, he was able to continue to believe both in Christ and in the Church."[11] Moreover, he had nothing particularly to lose in the sense of an academic or ecclesiastical position. After all, he was, in Marvin O'Connell's words, "a well-fixed, private layman, free to indulge his interests in a private manner and free also to encourage, cajole and admonish others less advantageously positioned than himself."[12] Despite the immanentist tendencies of some of those whom he knew, he never lost the sense of God's utter transcendence. Vatican Council II in many ways fulfilled a number of the dreams and aspirations von Hügel had had for the church.

The Three Dimensions of Religion

In his great work *The Mystical Element of Religion as Studied in Saint Catherine of Genoa and Her Friends,* a two-volume work of some 888 pages, von Hügel made his mark.[13] He maintained throughout his opus that religion is composed of three chief elements, or, from a Catholic point of view, we might say that there are three fundamental and essential elements to Catholicism: the institutional, the intellectual, and the mystical.

The institutional element has to do with external structures, offices, officers, and authority. However holy or devout or even ascetic a person might be, the institutional element is necessary. It is necessary because institutions provide the originating sources from which we absorb our beliefs, values, speech, and interests. Everything initially comes to us from outside ourselves, that is, from institutions. Von Hügel put it this way:

> Behind every saint stands another saint. In vain do all mystics, as such, vividly feel their experience to be utterly without human antecedent connection. Behind St. Paul stands the Jewish synagogue and the earthly Jesus….Here is the abiding right and need of the Church, as the fellowship and training-school of believers.[14]

The institutional element of Catholicism prevents the faith from becoming either too individualistic or, perhaps, from freezing into a negative other-worldliness. Von Hügel writes:

> Complete humility imperatively demands my continuous recognition of my own multifaceted need of my fellow-creatures, especially of those wiser and better than myself, and of my life-long need of training, discipline, incorporation. Full humility requires filial obedience and docility towards men and institutions, as well as fraternal give-and-take, paternal authority, and superintendence.[15]

As von Hügel understands it, we can no more do without institutions, including the institutional church, than we can do without the air we breathe. The question for von Hügel is *how* we breathe, but that takes us to the intellectual dimension.

"Scholarship was the path by which von Hügel responded to his vocation to become a saint."[16] The intellectual dimension of Catholicism obviously has to do with the life of the intellect, with reasoning, understanding, making sense of things for oneself. It is the business of asking questions and seeking answers. As we attempt as Catholics to make sense of ourselves and our surrounding diachronically through our inherited tradition, and synchronically through the making of the tradition that is the church today, we will find a variety of approaches to and interpretations of our rites, beliefs, and moral values—in a word, our self-understanding. At times, this vast and diverse school of interpretation that is the church will be conflictual, but "there are no shortcuts or final solutions."[17] Von Hügel valued enormously the intellectual life, the *quaerens intellectum* of the *fides*.

This was especially the case with the study of scripture. Von Hügel has been described recently as "an intellectual clearinghouse and pivot for the dissemination and stimulation of biblical scholarship among modern-minded Catholics in Europe."[18] His earliest interest in biblical studies was in textual criticism. Thus, he was in touch with John Wordsworth (later Bishop Wordsworth) of Oxford, who had been preparing a critical text of the Vulgate. He was familiar with Tischendorff's critical editions of the Greek New Testament, having begun the study of the Greek New Testament and various scholarly commentaries in 1879. He started to learn Hebrew in 1890, when he was thirty-eight years old, and in 1895, while he was in Rome, he took lessons in Aramaic from Ignazio Guidi of the Urban College. He recommended to Fr. Tyrrell that he learn German so as to profit from the work of German scholars that remained untranslated into English, for example, the work of Rudolf Eucken. In fact, Tyrrell did exactly that.

Hans Rollmann provides us with information concerning von Hügel's study methods, based on a close examination of the baron's library, now housed at St. Andrews University Library, Scotland: "Von Hügel not only underlined significant passages, he also developed a system of marginal outlines and annotations and furnished on the inside covers four types of comments: *Annotanda, Criticanda, Admiranda, and Corrigenda*."[19] His desire was not simply to be current with biblical scholarship himself but also to advance the cause of biblical studies in the church. In 1911 he published his article on the Fourth Gospel in the *Encyclopedia Britannica* (11th edition), his "most serious exegetical contribution."[20] Here was a man who knew experientially what the Canadian Jesuit Bernard Lonergan aptly called "the unrestricted desire to understand." Yet von Hügel never regarded it as sufficient. As with the institutional dimension, the intellectual dimension does not stand on its own but gives way to the mystical dimension.

The mystical dimension of Catholicism is expressed in worship, in prayer, and in an explicit sense of being in God's presence. Ellen Leonard, a close student of both modernism and von Hügel, writes: "His diaries reveal a man for whom the liturgical life of the Church provided a framework for his daily activities."[21] For von Hügel, the term *mysticism* does not refer primarily to those individuals gifted with an extraordinary experience of the supernatural; rather, the mystical exists "in some form and degree in every mind."[22] In virtue of being human, then, everyone has an openness to God, a graced orientation to the divine, and "mysticism" is its cultivation. The most compelling description of it in von Hügel is this: "An absolute abidingness, pure simultaneity, eternity, in God...stand out in man's deepest consciousness, with even painful contrast, against all mere succession, all sheer flux and change."[23]

Creative Tension

Each of the three dimensions must be kept permanently in play in order to achieve some increasing degree of balance and to avoid the manifold corporate and personal problems that are consequent on imbalance. Each of the three dimensions also has its own particular temptation. The temptation of the institutional dimension is *coercive power,* forcing and requiring both conformity and uniformity. The temptation of the intellectual dimension is *rationalism,* the (implicit) assumption that the human intellect (and, finally *my* intellect) establishes the parameters of truth. The temptation of the mystical dimension is *superstition,* a quasi-magical sense of the divine presence.

The temptation of each element of Catholicism is to think of itself as the whole. If the ecclesial temptation is to absolutize one dimension at the expense of the others, it is no less the case in the individual human soul. Keeping all three permanently in play leads to tension, as von Hügel notes: "the joint presence of three such disparate elements ever involves tension of a fruitful or dangerous kind."[24] Maturity, both ecclesial and personal, consists in living with this tension without the premature erasure of any of the three elements. Individual people will in their own persons tend to identify with one or other of the three dimensions for a host of reasons, social and psychological. That is unavoidable, given our originating and formative circumstances in life. However, to permit one dimension to eliminate the others will lead ineluctably to narrowness of vision and temperamental imbalance, not only in one's own life but in one's ministry to others. Maturing in faith is dependent on living with the creative tension generated by the three elements so as to produce *sanitas,* health.

The Three Dimensions and the Life Cycle

The three dimensions of Catholicism are necessary ultimately because they correspond to stages in growth in the life cycle, according to von Hügel. The child's first contact with religion is with the *institution,* with the external plane of religion, best characterized as "institutional, imitative affiliation." The appeal of religion "would generally have been externally interpreted to us by some particular men or women, a Mother, Nurse, Father, Teacher, Cleric, who themselves would generally have belonged to some more or less well-defined traditional, institutional religion."[25] As changes come about with the onset of adolescence, when the person moves from an imposed set of beliefs and values to a more self-imposed set, religion necessarily takes on a more *intellectual* character: "the facts seem to clamor for reasons to back them, against the other hostile facts and appearances….Here it is the reasoning, argumentative, abstractive side of human nature that begins to come into play."[26] With the emergence of mature adulthood, the *mystical* develops:

> Man's emotional and volitional, his ethical and spiritual powers, are now in ever fuller motion, and they are met and fed by the third side of religion, the experimental and mystical. Here religion is rather felt than seen or reasoned about, is loved and lived rather than analyzed, is action and power, rather than either external fact or intellectual verification.[27]

It is not the case, however, that one grows out of one stage or element so that it is replaced by another. The three stages may be chronologically sequential, but they are at the same time cumulative; that is to say, one depends on the others in such a fashion as finally to be fully interdependent. Just as adults in the life cycle will experience tension, so also does the religious person in terms of their religious faith. Von Hügel believed firmly in "the spiritual benefits of friction."[28]

The finest example of the attempt to maintain balance in the three elements of Catholicism in von Hügel's own life is afforded by Abbot Cuthbert Butler, OSB, of Downside Abbey. Abbot Butler, noted author of works on Vatican Council I and western mysticism. Abbot Butler remembered long walks with von Hügel on Hampstead Heath when their discussions would be deep and wide-ranging, and he says: "And we always returned home by the little Catholic Church in Holly Place— it was [von Hügel's] daily practice—and went in for a long visit to the Blessed Sacrament; and there I would watch him sitting, the great deep eyes on the tabernacle, the whole being rapt in an absorption of prayer, devotion, contemplation. Those who have not seen him so know only half the man."[29]

Conclusion

The quest for balance will be coterminous with the life of the person, ending only with the Beatific Vision. But von Hügel's formula seems to offer the contemporary Catholic success as one moves toward integral balance in one's formation. As the Catholic enfleshes in one's own person the tensive balance between the institutional, the intellectual, and the mystical dimensions of Catholicism, the individual's efforts become invitational to others to seek after the same kind of balance, or wholeness. Balance—wholeness, or *sanitas*—is infectious in the best sense of the word.

Bibliography

De la Bedoyere, Michael. *The Life of Baron von Hügel.* London: J. M. Dent, 1951.

Leonard, Ellen M. *Creative Tension: The Spiritual Legacy of Friedrich von Hügel.* Scranton, PA: University of Scranton Press, 1997.

Trevor, Meriol. *Prophets and Guardians: Renewal and Tradition in the Church.* London/Sydney/Toronto: Hollis and Carter, 1969.

Whelan, Joseph, SJ. *The Spirituality of Friedrich von Hügel.* London: Collins, 1971.

Notes

1. Ellen M. Leonard, *Creative Tension: The Spiritual Legacy of Friedrich von Hügel* (Scranton, PA: University of Scranton Press, 1997), 91.

2. Alec R. Vidler, *A Variety of Catholic Modernists* (Cambridge: Cambridge University Press, 1970), 113.

3. Ibid., 122–23.

4. Nicholas L. A. Lash, *Easter in Ordinary: Reflections on Human Experience and the Knowledge of God* (Charlottesville: University Press of Virginia, 1988), 175.

5. See Michael de la Bedoyere, *The Life of Baron von Hügel* (London: J. M. Dent, 1951), 18.

6. Meriol Trevor, *Prophets and Guardians: Renewal and Tradition in the Church* (London/Sydney/Toronto: Hollis and Carter, 1969), 49.

7. Ibid., 124.

8. Ibid., 51–52.

9. Friedrich von Hügel, *The Reality of God and Religion and Agnosticism,* ed. Edmund Gardner, (London: J. M. Dent, 1931).

10. Trevor, *Prophets and Guardians,* 47.

11. Ibid., 65.

12. Marvin R. O'Connell, *Critics on Trial: An Introduction to the Catholic Modernist Crisis* (Washington, DC: Catholic University of America Press, 1994), 51.

13. Friedrich von Hügel, *The Mystical Element of Religion as Studied in Saint Catherine of Genoa and Her Friends* (London: J. M. Dent, 1908).

14. Friedrich von Hügel, *Essays and Addresses* (London: J. M. Dent, 1921), 1:293.

15. Ibid., 1:264.

16. Leonard, *Creative Tension,* 142.

17. Nicholas Lash, "The Difficulty of Making Sense," *New Blackfriars* 70 (February 1989): 77. Professor Lash is a von Hügel devotee.

18. Hans Rollmann, "Baron Friedrich Von Hügel and the Conveyance of German Protestant Biblical Criticism in Roman Catholic Modernism," in *Biblical Studies and the Shifting of Paradigms, 1850–1914,* ed. H. G. Reventlow and W. Farmer (Sheffield: Sheffield Academic Press, 1995), 197–98.

19. Ibid., 201.

20. Ibid., 212.

21. Leonard, *Creative Tension,* 28.

22. Friedrich von Hügel, *Selected Letters,* ed. B. Holland (London: J. M. Dent, 1927), 84.

23. Friedrich von Hügel, *Eternal Life: A Study of Its Implications and Applications* (Edinburgh: T. & T. Clark, 1912), 365.

24. Von Hügel, *Mystical Element,* 1:53.

25. Ibid., 1:51.

26. Ibid., 1:52.

27. Ibid., 1:53.

28. The phrase comes from Gabriel Daly, *Transcendence and Immanence* (Oxford: Clarendon Press, 1980), 136.

29. Cited in Joseph Whelan, *The Spirituality of Friedrich Von Hügel* (London: Collins, 1971), 16.

10
POPE PIUS X (1835–1914)

The twentieth century papacy began, as was appropriate in the age of the common man, with a peasant pope, the first for three centuries, Giuseppe Sarto.

—Eamon Duffy[1]

Giuseppe Sarto was born on June 2, 1835, in the village of Riese in Venetia. His father was the village postman and his mother a seamstress. After his ordination to the priesthood in 1858, Sarto spent nine years as a curate in Tombolo and then eight years as a pastor in Salzano. He had solid pastoral experience.

He was named bishop of Mantua in 1884, at the time not an easy responsibility. In 1871, Canon Roberto Ardigo, a well-known priest, lost his faith and became a professor of philosophy. During Sarto's time Giovanni Grisanti, archpriest of Rovere, a principal town in the diocese, left the priesthood and became a Protestant. The new bishop, during his nine-year stay in this diocese, threw himself into catechetical work. In 1889 he participated in the first National Catechetical Conference in Piacenza and proposed the use of a uniform catechetical text. The proposal was accepted by the conference and sent on to Rome. When the opportunity presented itself, he made himself rector of his diocesan seminary, appointing himself also as professor of philosophy, thus ensuring that the seminarians were taught Thomism. In 1893, Pope Leo XIII made him a cardinal and three days later named him patriarch of Venice. Political machinations prevented him entering his new see until November 1894. In Venice, Sarto continued his interest in catechetics, showed interest in church music, and encouraged frequent reception of the Eucharist.

It is said that his neighbor-bishop asked Sarto in French in the 1903 conclave following the death of Leo XIII, whether he was an Italian bishop. Sarto replied that he was unable to speak French, to which the Frenchman replied in Latin: "It is not possible for you to be pope; a pope must be able to speak French." "Perfectly true, your eminence," responded Sarto, "I am not a possible pope. Thank God."[2] Sarto was elected, taking the name of Pius X. French was the language of diplomacy at the time, and Sarto was not at all fluent in French, though he could get by, and, like popes John Paul I and John Paul II and Benedict XVI, he had never held a formal diplomatic post. Eamon Duffy writes: "Not one of his nineteenth-century predecessors had been a parish priest. Sarto, even as bishop of Mantua and patriarch of Venice, had never really been anything else."[3]

A parish priest Sarto may have been, but taking the name of Pius was quite deliberate, as he saw himself in an adversarial position vis-à-vis the modern world, maintaining Pio Nono's ultramontanism. Carlo Falconi points out that "even physically, and in his whole bearing," the similarity to Pio Nono was noticeable.[4] Pius X was to write: "When we speak of the Vicar of Christ, we must not quibble, we must obey: we must not…evaluate his judgments, criticize his directions, lest we do injury to Jesus Christ himself. Society is sick…the one hope, the one remedy, is the Pope."[5]

As pope, Pius X contrasts strongly with his immediate predecessor, Leo XIII. Leo loved pomp and ceremonial and being carried around; Pius hated it. Leo let visitors remain on their knees during private, papal audiences; Pius seated them. He abolished the 260-year-old tradition of popes eating alone and discouraged the custom of clapping when he entered St. Peter's Basilica. Leo was fond of an entourage of guards, chaplains, and attendants, even on a private walk. Pius's preference was for a solitary walk, or with a secretary. Leo never wore a watch, but Pius used a cheap watch, valued because it had been at his mother's deathbed. Leo used a quill pen, especially for more important documents, but Pius used an ordinary pen, sometimes cleaning the nib on the side of his pontifical robes. In twenty-five years Leo never spoke a word to his private coachman, whereas Pius talked to and joked with everyone. Owen Chadwick continues the contrast humorously: "He hated his toe being kissed and avoided it when he could. He was a man of compassion with no time for shams."[6] One of his innovations as pope was personally to hold a catechism session for the public every Sunday afternoon, continuing the strong catechetical interest of his days as a bishop.

The French Problem

Relations between the church and France had never been easy since the French Revolution. Ardent Catholics were too often right-wing monarchists; zealous republicans were too often left-wing anticlericals. Leo XIII had tried to promote better relations through his not-very-successful encouraging of French Catholics to go some way to supporting the republican government. Perhaps because of his lack of formal diplomatic experience, Pius tended to be more confrontational. Though by no means entirely Pius's fault, relations between the church and France came to a standstill in 1905.

There were two incidents by which Pius's actions contributed to the rift. First, Pius demanded the resignation of two French bishops who were accused of freemasonry and immorality. The very anticlerical French premier, Émile Combes, refused to permit this, arguing that this amounted to papal interference in the rights of the French government. Second, in 1904, when the president of France was making a courteous return visit to King Victor Emmanuel III of Italy, Pius refused the president an audience. This, of course, reflected the difficulty of the Roman question, but there was more to it. The tension continued to mount between the

Vatican and France, culminating in a law of 1905 that abolished the Concordat of 1801. Church and state were now entirely separate. No longer would clergy stipends be paid by the state. Church buildings and property passed into the hands of the state, to be administered for the church by associations of laity known as *Associations Cultuelles.* The French episcopate, in a very delicate and difficult situation, sought to find a realistic compromise, or at least a *modus agendi* with the state that would be acceptable to the Vatican. Pius would have nothing to do with anything that smacked of compromise.

Reaction to Modernism

For an understanding of the complex phenomenon of modernism, one should refer to chapter 8 above. Here our concern will be with the church's reaction to modernism. On July 3, 1907, the Holy Office published the decree *Lamentabili,* containing some sixty-five extracts from modernist writing, and especially from the works of Alfred Loisy. This was followed on September 8 by the encyclical *Pascendi.* The modernists were seen in extremely negative light, "feigning a love for the Church," and "vaunt[ing] themselves as reformers of the Church...assailing all that is most sacred in the work of Christ."[7] This is very strong language indeed, and, while doubtless there were men of acerbity among the modernists, this does not apply to many good people who suffered under this denunciation. Falconi sadly comments, "The Church was showing a quite new aspect of itself, devouring its own children...."[8]

The philosophical foundation of the heresy is seen in agnosticism, a system of thought that confines human reason to empirical data and phenomena (par. 6). Another central principle is "immanence," the rooting of religion in "sentiment, a movement of the heart" (par. 7). To this is also allied a *theological* immanence, that is to say, the immanence of God within humankind, expressed externally in religious dogma. This latter

certainly has a Loisy-feel to it. Perhaps we can see in immanence and in religious immanence something of the religious
epistemology of Friedrich Schleiermacher, so widespread in the
nineteenth century but doubtfully of overwhelming influence
among Catholic theologians. For Schleiermacher, the roots of
religion are to be found in the feeling of absolute dependence,
innate in all human beings, and religious doctrine is but a conceptual explication of that sense. *Pascendi* addresses a central
tendency in nineteenth-century theology, but not particularly
widespread among Catholics. Modernism is "the synthesis of all
heresies" (par. 39). To counteract it, the encyclical proposes a
series of measures: the study of scholastic philosophy, careful
diligence in examining and selecting candidates for ordination;
episcopal vigilance over publications; censorship; careful over-
sight over congresses; and diocesan watch committees.[9]

Aidan Nichols, OP, writes carefully that "[t]he Roman
response [to modernism], despite the presence of a canonized
saint on the chair of Peter [Pius X Sarto], left something to be
desired."[10] Alec Vidler is harsher:

> [He] did not take the name of "Pius" for nothing. He
> stood for a reversion to the conservative intransigence
> of Pius IX. He regarded it as his mission to stamp out
> all dangerous thinking in the Church, and had the
> power to do so....It is hardly an exaggeration to say
> that a reign of doctrinal terror was maintained until
> the death of Pius X in 1914, and even then was only
> gradually relaxed.[11]

Between the views of Nichols and Vidler one recognizes that
there was a problem that was not well handled. It seems clear that
Pius had no close awareness or understanding of all that was
going on with "modernist" theology and views. His was essentially the response of a conservative pastor, concerned for the well-
being of his people. Nevertheless, he had power and he used it,
and not always well. During the process for his beatification, his

private secretary, Monsignor Pescini, acknowledged under oath: "The great struggle undertaken and conducted with such energy and efficiency against Modernism was personally directed and sustained by Pius X despite considerable opposition and forces."[12] Seminary professors judged to be modernist were replaced, and a climate of fear and suspicion arose in the church.

Owen Chadwick writes that "Pius X needed a confidant who could tell him how to eradicate the treachery which he believed that he faced. He found Monsignor Umberto Benigni."[13] Monsignor Benigni established the Sodalitium Pianum/League of St. Pius V. Through this secret society of informers, he discovered modernists, or those suspected of modernism, everywhere. He created a special set of codes for his correspondents, for example, referring to Pius as "Mama." A virtual witch-hunt of Catholic intellectuals took place. "It was not only modernists who were under suspicion, it was anyone scholarly."[14]

All kinds of good, honest scholars found themselves under suspicion. One of the victims of the Sodalitium Pianum was a young professor of church history at the seminary in Bergamo, Angelo Roncalli, the future Pope John XXIII. Roncalli had been denounced to Rome for recommending that his students read Louis Duchesne's *Early History of the Church*. The story is told of Giorgio LaPiana, who later became a professor at Harvard, that he was traveling as a young priest on the train from Sicily to Rome. A traveling companion with whom he fell into conversation revealed his sympathies with modernism. LaPiana must have shown some degree of empathy in the conversation because some days later he was reprimanded and sent back to his diocese.[15] In his Lenten Letter of 1915 Cardinal Désiré Joseph Mercier, the Louvain Thomist scholar under Leo XIII and now Archbishop of Malines, who had himself been suspected of modernism, wrote of this witch-hunt:

> Modernism had indeed drawn some impetuous spirits, more courageous in words than deeds, into violent

and insidious personal controversy....Petty scribes or worthless journalists, they excommunicated all those unwilling to pass beneath the Caudine forks of their integralism. Sincere hearts were troubled by unrest: the more honest consciences suffered in silence.[16]

Pope Benedict XV, Pius's successor, got rid of Benigni, who ended his life as a fascist. It would probably be too strong to claim that this condemnation of modernism killed Catholic scholarship as such, but it did put severe restrictions on creative theological thinking. Moreover, it led to a climate in the church in which critical thinking of any kind was frowned upon. Catholics, rather, were to accept the faith of the whole church, what might be called the "integral faith," and so, "integrist" or "integralist" became a term for virtually total and complete and unthinking docility. "'Real' Catholics were 'integralists,' accepting as a package deal everything the pope taught, not picking and choosing in the 'pride and curiosity' of their intellect."[17]

Theology and the Life of the Church

Pius set in motion the codification of canon law for the first time, a mere eight months after his election. The practical aspects of canon law appealed to him, and it is said that as a priest in Tombolo he divided his leisure reading between the *Summa Theologiae* of Aquinas, and Gratian's *Decretals*. While patriarch of Venice, he instituted a chair of canon law with the right to confer degrees in the discipline. He wanted the ordinary priest to know his way around canon law so as to be of real assistance to his people. The task of codification was entrusted to Cardinal Pietro Gasparri, who had been a professor of canon law at the Institut Catholique de Paris for over twenty years and was the author of a number of standard Latin texts on the laws of marriage, ordination, and the Eucharist. Gasparri was assisted in this enterprise by the young Eugenio Pacelli, later to become Pope Pius XII. Before Pius X died, the code was almost complete and was finally promulgated by Pope Benedict XV in 1917. It made access to canon law much easier for diocesan administrators and canonists.

Chadwick maintains that "[The Code of Canon Law] was also the legal sanction of the centralization that took place during the nineteenth century."[18] The principal example he provides is the appointment of bishops in canon 329.2, "The Pope nominates bishops freely." To us this seems self-evident, but it was not the universal custom in the church, even in the nineteenth century, so that Chadwick can comment: "The canon in the codex was aspiration more than reality."[19] Perhaps, but now that aspiration was law in the church, and a law that was to be practiced and held to. In a sense, there was something of a tension between Pius's pastoral side and the juridical ecclesiology that was to be found in the new code. Falconi writes:

> Pius X's chief responsibility in relation to the Code of Canon Law undoubtedly lies in its pervading conception of the Church and of its rigid hierarchical structure, constituting the most solemn ratification of the ecclesiology that culminated in the nineteenth century with the first Vatican Council and the encyclicals of Leo XIII: thus demonstrating incidentally, his unawareness of the strident contradiction between his own work of evangelical reform and the suffocating effects of legal curbs and checks not sufficiently attuned to purely spiritual needs.[20]

"Strident contradiction" may be too harsh, but there is certainly tension.

In 1909 Pius established the Pontifical Biblical Institute to promote the scientific study of scripture. In this respect, he aligned himself with the "progressivism" of Leo XIII. Again like Leo, he upheld and promoted the study of St. Thomas Aquinas in ecclesiastical schools.

His consistent interest in church music led him to publish the *motu proprio Tra le sollecitudini* in 1903. He was utterly opposed to musical theatricality in church, "in which the church became almost an extension of the opera house, with worshippers paying more attention to the choir than to the altar, waiting for the moment when their idol would appear in a cavatina or duet, for all the world as if they were on the stage."[21] Instead, Pius wanted traditional sacred music that would lift the mind and heart to God. *Tra le sollecitudini* provided norms for sacred music and encouraged Gregorian chant, and used of the liturgy the phrase that was to become famous in Vatican II's Constitution on the Sacred Liturgy, "full, conscious, and active participation." Chadwick draws a parallel between Leo XIII and Pius X: "As Pope Leo XIII made St. Thomas Aquinas the key to philosophical theology, so Pius X made the Gregorian chant the perfection of church music."[22]

Up to the end of the nineteenth century, many Mass-going Catholics did not receive holy communion except a few times a year. This was largely a consequence of Jansenism. Jansenists encouraged very careful preparation for holy communion, including sacramental confession. Leo XIII encouraged more frequent communion, but it was Pius X who seriously tried to achieve this. In a series of twelve statements issued between 1905 and 1907, the pope encouraged people to receive the Eucharist, even on a daily basis—something St. Thérèse of Lisieux had wished for but not experienced in her lifetime. Through his 1910 decree *Quam Singulari,* Pius brought down the age for first communion to the age of reason and ordered parish clergy to spend one hour every Sunday catechizing children. "These acts of Pius X amounted to a revolution in worshipping practices. Historians, in hindsight, if asked which act of which pope did most to affect the Church since 1800, would put their finger on this change of 1905-1906, the encouragement of frequent, even daily communion, and the receiving of it by children."[23]

Conclusion

Pope Pius X was both a reformer and a reactionary, something of a prophet at times, but with a strong custodial sense. The year 1910 was the occasion of the first International Missionary Conference in Edinburgh, the first major twentieth-century step toward the establishment of ecumenism as central to the Christian enterprise. There was no encouragement under Pius for Catholics to participate in ecumenism in any sense of the word. Indeed, in that very same year, 1910, Pius refused an audience to former U.S. President Theodore Roosevelt, because Roosevelt intended to speak in the Methodist Church in Rome. Pusillanimity, such as this is, may not simply be accounted for in terms of historical context and circumstances. Yet, on the other hand, Pius was deeply grieved at the outbreak of the Great War in 1914, so grieved that many said he died of a broken heart. He published an exhortation, *Dum Europa fere,* on August 2 and died some eighteen days later. Does ecclesially established sanctity always correlate with human consistency, and what does it mean to be consistent?

Bibliography

Chadwick, Owen. *A History of the Popes 1830–1914.* Oxford: Clarendon Press, 1998.

Duffy, Eamon. *Saints and Sinners: A History of the Popes.* Rev. ed. New Haven/London: Yale University Press, 2001.

Falconi, Carlo. *The Popes in the Twentieth Century.* London: Weidenfeld and Nicholson, 1967.

Notes

1. Eamon Duffy, *Saints and Sinners: A History of the Popes,* 2nd ed. (New Haven/London: Yale University Press, 2001), 320.

2. Owen Chadwick, *A History of the Popes 1830–1914* (Oxford: Clarendon Press, 1998), 337.

3. Duffy, *Saints and Sinners,* 320.

4. Carlo Falconi, *The Popes in the Twentieth Century* (London: Weidenfeld and Nicholson, 1967), 15.

5. I. Giordani, *Pius X, A Country Priest* (Milwaukee: Bruce, 1954), 47.

6. Chadwick, *History of the Popes 1830–1914,* 345.

7. Pascendi, par. 2, cited from *The Papal Encyclicals 1903–1939,* ed. Claudia Carlen IHM (Washington, DC: A Consortium Book, McGrath Publishing, 1981), 71.

8. Falconi, *Popes in the Twentieth Century,* 35.

9. *Papal Encyclicals,* ed. Carlen, 92–96.

10. Aidan Nichols, OP, *Catholic Thought since the Enlightenment: A Survey,* (Leominster, UK: Gracewing, 1998), 88.

11. Alec R. Vidler, *20th Century Defenders of the Faith* (London: SCM Press, 1965), 36.

12. Falconi, *Popes in the Twentieth Century,* 53.

13. Chadwick, *History of the Popes 1830–1914,* 356.

14. Ibid., 357.

15. The episode, with sources, is recounted in Falconi, *Popes in the Twentieth Century,* 41.

16. Cited in Falconi, *Popes in the Twentieth Century,* 38.

17. Duffy, *Saints and Sinners,* 329.

18. Chadwick, *History of the Popes 1830–1914,* 360.

19. Ibid.

20. Falconi, *Popes in the Twentieth Century,* 26–27.

21. Ibid., 22.

22. Chadwick, *History of the Popes 1830-1914,* 364.

23. Ibid., 362.

11
THÉRÈSE MARTIN (1873–1897) AND MAUDE PETRE (1863–1942)

One of the last acts of the twentieth-century papacy was to take up the name of a middle-class girl who lived all her short life in a couple of French provincial towns and declare its bearer a doctor of the Church.

—Aidan Nichols, OP[1]

Some Modernists gave up faith for history; some gave up history for faith. Some sought a method of evasion in a philosophy of pure symbolism. Some kept both faith and problem.

—Maude Petre[2]

Some may be aggrieved that this chapter contains two very different women, a saint and a suspected modernist, Thérèse of Lisieux and Maude Petre. Is it not fundamentally disrespectful to place the saint alongside an alleged heretic? That judgment is too unsubtle. St. Thérèse of Lisieux has become one of the most popular saints of all time, commanding the devotion, for example, of the singer Edith Piaf, brought up in a brothel in Lisieux and not particularly active as a Catholic. Thérèse has been the subject of over nine hundred biographies, almost one a month since her death. Very few people, on the other hand, will ever have heard of Maude Petre, perhaps the first of modern women theologians, and yet her inclusion in this chapter points to the sheer breadth of Catholicism. Maude was ten years older than Thérèse, and lived forty-five years after

Thérèse had died. Although Maude certainly was a modernist of sorts, she was never personally condemned for heresy.

Thérèse of Lisieux

Life

As with Cardinal Newman and Maude Petre, we possess a great deal of information about Thérèse Martin. There are forty-seven photographs of Thérèse, almost all of them taken by her sister, both sibling and fellow Carmelite, Céline, who had become an accomplished photographer before she entered Carmel. In fact, no other saint is so well documented, with an autobiography, a voluminous correspondence, a large body of poetry and playlets, the firsthand testimony of contemporary witnesses, and finally these forty-seven photographs.

Marie Françoise Thérèse Martin, the youngest of nine children born to Louis and Zélie Martin, was born in Alençon, France on January 2, 1873. Both parents were very devout, and both had contemplated the religious life. A sickly child, Thérèse had to be boarded with a wet nurse for the first year of her life. In 1877 her mother died of breast cancer at the age of forty-seven. Her mother's premature death was, understandably, a traumatic experience for her. In 1881 the Martin family moved to Lisieux, so that they might be closer to Zélie's brother and sister-in-law, the Guérins. Thérèse attended the Benedictine Abbey School as a day student. Although she was a bright and receptive student, she was also shy and found school life difficult. In 1883 she became strangely ill over a period of about three months, "strangely" because the illness was a mixture of convulsions, hallucinations, and comas. For all practical purposes Thérèse suffered a complete nervous breakdown. It was probably brought on by the sudden departure of her sister Pauline for the Carmel in Lisieux. Pauline had been her second mother for almost six years, and now Pauline too was torn away from her as her natural mother had been.

At Christmas 1886, Thérèse experienced her "conversion," a new religious maturity. When she and Céline returned with their father from midnight Mass and entered their living room, under the chimney were her slippers, filled with presents, a custom that had continued ever since she had been a little girl. She was delighted as usual, of course, but her father, thinking that she should have outgrown this custom, was somewhat annoyed. As Thérèse went upstairs, she heard him say to Céline, "Fortunately, this will be the last year!" He did not intend her to hear the remark, but Céline saw that she did and knew the effect that it would have on her. She went to comfort Thérèse, but Thérèse, forcing back her tears, picked up the slippers and brought them to her father. With excitement and joy she tore the wrappings from her presents and thanked him for them one by one. Forgetting his displeasure, Louis was soon laughing with her and enjoying the little ritual as much as he ever did. From that day until the end of her life, she never cried over minor issues again.

Her two sisters Pauline and Marie entered the Carmel of Lisieux, Marie (1860–1940) in 1886 (Sister Marie of the Sacred Heart), and Pauline (1861–1951) in 1882 (Mother Agnes of Jesus). Thérèse applied to enter the Carmel when she was only fourteen. Abbé Delatroette, the ecclesiastical superior of the convent, advised her to wait until she was twenty-one. Thérèse, accompanied by her father, petitioned her ordinary, Bishop Flavien-Abel-Antonin Hugonin for early admission, but received much the same answer. Shortly afterwards, she went on a diocesan pilgrimage to Rome with her father for the jubilee of Pope Leo XIII. Aidan Nichols notes: "On arrival at Rome, she expressed her opinion that the pope was so old as to be almost dead. (He was to outlive her by six years.)"[3] In the general audience, the pilgrims were to be presented to Pope Leo XIII individually, but they were instructed that they must not speak because the delay might tire the aging pope. When

Thérèse's turn came to kneel before him, she took his two hands in hers and again made her plea for an early entry to Carmel. Leo turned to the bishop's vicar-general to be sure of what she was asking. The vicar-general, annoyed that Thérèse had broken the rule of silence, explained that the superiors were considering the matter. "Then do what the superiors decide," the pope said. "Oh, Holy Father, she urged, "if you say yes, everyone else will too." The pope gently placed his finger on her lips and blessed her. "If God wills it, you will enter, my child." Thérèse was carried off in tears by two Roman guards.

In fact, Thérèse entered the Carmel of Lisieux early, on April 9, 1888, at fifteen years of age, and spent the remaining nine and a half years of her life there as Sister Thérèse of the Child Jesus and the Holy Face. "Of the Child Jesus" was given her at the time she entered Carmel; "the Holy Face" was the devotion she chose for herself when she received the veil at the age of sixteen. Behind this devotion lies the apocryphal story of Veronica wiping the face of Jesus on his way to Calvary, the face of the suffering Christ. Theologian Hans Urs von Balthasar comments as follows:

> That image which she placed at the centre of her entire devotion; the face of our Lord suffering, with his eyelids closed. Her whole life in Christ is concentrated into her devotion to the Holy Face; unwaveringly, she gazes upon God in the extremity of his love, gazing on his face where the eternal light seems to have been extinguished and yet is most transparent, streaming irresistibly from beneath the closed lids...the Holy Face...is for her the direct revelation and vision of the divine countenance....She gazes entranced upon those downcast eyes; everything is centered there."[4]

The Holy Face of Jesus also reminded her of her dear father, Louis. Just three months after her entry to Carmel, her father began to change. Arteriosclerosis of the brain caused memory loss, mood swings, and an urge to run away from home. He meandered from home on a number of occasions, and the family had no sense of his whereabouts—that is, until he became aware of it and contacted them. Eventually he had to be placed in a mental institution in Caen, Bon Sauveur. There he was to stay for almost four years. Shortly after his release from Bon Sauveur, Louis died in the arms of his daughter Céline. The townspeople of Lisieux put it about that Thérèse had broken her father's heart with her unflinching and somewhat premature desire to be a Carmelite, which caused much personal grief and suffering for her. Describing Thérèse's devotion to the Holy Face, one commentator, Ida Goerres, talks about not only Christ but also her beloved father, Louis Martin: "The face of the person she loved most on earth was now for ever deprived of sanity and transformed into the frightful mask of living death....With the obsessiveness of grief she pondered on the meaning of this trial which had befallen so faithful a servant of God."[5] She prayed to Christ as the Holy Face. She wrote hymns and poems about it, meditated on it, and during her last illness she had the picture of the Holy Face on the curtain near her bed so that she could always see it.[6] Ida Goerres tells of an experience of encountering Thérèse's own face at a German Catholic Youth meeting. A student brought out this picture of Thérèse from his wallet, and showed it to the others, including Ida, and someone in the group remarked something like, "It's almost like the face of a female Christ."[7]

The Carmel of Lisieux, like any other human family, was far from serene. For most of the time Thérèse's superior was Mother Marie de Gonzague, *une dame formidable,* and there was the usual and normal round of internal politics. Thérèse abstained from the inner politics of the convent and concentrated on her own inner life of prayer. In 1893 she was appointed acting mistress of novices and held this position for the last four years of her life. It was during this time that she articulated her "Little Way" of love.

On October 15, 1895, Thérèse received her first letter from Maurice Bellière, a seminarian who, in his own words, was having "a hard time absorbing the spirit of the Church and holding himself to all the demands of the seminary rule."[8] Bellière had written to the Carmel in Lisieux and had asked the mother superior to appoint a Carmelite to pray for him. Thérèse was that Carmelite, and, though they never met, they exchanged twenty-one letters. In these letters Thérèse supported Maurice by offering advice and sharing her great spirit with him. Really, Maurice was the priest brother she never had, and she often referred to him as "my dear, little brother." She continued to write in support of him even during her final illness. Here was no sickly introvert who could not see beyond the confines of her own very painful suffering.

That suffering came from tuberculosis, the first manifestations of which were seen in 1895. During her final illness, she was often fatigued, racked with pain, and plunged into temptation against faith. She wrote out the Apostles' Creed in her own blood, and pinned it beneath her habit, close to her heart. This trial of faith was to last some eighteen months. Her final words before death were: "Oh, how I love you!…My God….How I love you!" She had a vision of God, the only vision she ever had, and it was to last only a few moments. Then she sank back on the pillow, her eyes closed. It was September 30, 1895, and she was twenty-four years old. In 1997 Pope John Paul II made her a doctor of the church.

Spirituality

Thérèse's writings are extensive. In point of fact, she wrote more prose than St. John of the Cross, and three times as much poetry—astonishing given the fact that he lived until he was forty-nine and she died at twenty-four. Here Thérèse's spiritual doctrine and experience will be treated under three headings.

First, the vocation to love. Meditation on the great Pauline texts of 1 Corinthians 12–13 brought Thérèse to see the many different charisms given by God, but the question emerged, Which charism was hers as a contemplative? She came to the conclusion that her charism was "To be love in the heart of the church":

> I finally had rest. Concerning the mystical body of the Church, I had not recognized myself in any of the members described by St. Paul, or rather I desired to see myself in them *all*. *Charity* gave me the key to my *vocation*. I understood that if the Church had a body composed of different members, the most necessary and most noble of all could not be lacking to it, and so I understood that the Church *had a Heart and that this Heart* was BURNING WITH LOVE....Then, in the excess of my delirious joy, I cried out: O Jesus, my Love...my *vocation* at last I have found it...MY VOCATION IS LOVE![9]

There is nothing easy about this love. Thérèse writes in a letter to Maurice Bellière: "To love Jesus, the more one is weak, without desires and without virtues, the more one is suitable for the operations of [God's] consuming and transforming love. It is confidence and nothing but confidence that must lead us to love."[10] This is a "consuming and transforming love," a love that makes demands even as it becomes effective in the Christian life. This "Little Way of love" opened up to Thérèse possibilities that were realistic, even though in their own way difficult. Bishop Patrick Ahern writes: "She soon gave up [great penances], content to offer God the small sacrifices which came in the routine of community life, the little occasions to be kind to others, the apostolate of the smile when smiling at another was the last thing she felt like doing."[11] Hers was a love that cast out fear from faith. Jansenism, with its fear of God and rather pessimistic view of humankind, still made its presence felt in France and northern Europe, but not for Thérèse. "How can I fear a God," she said, "Who is nothing but mercy and love?"

God asks from us that we approach his loving embrace with the confidence of children. Of Thérèse in her own life, Bishop Ahern says, "With a single blow she broke the chains of Jansenism."[12] The Martin family was anything but Jansenist. They were celebratory and fun-loving and had a love of frequent reception of the Eucharist, all decidedly anti-Jansenist traits.[13] The Martins knew that God was Love.

In a letter to Maurice Bellière, Thérèse talks of God's love as like an elevator! "I understand better than ever how much your soul is the sister of my own, since it is called to life itself up to God by the ELEVATOR of love and not climb the hard stairway of fear."[14] Though we may be weak, God will come down like the elevator, pick up his child in his arms, and carry him up to where he is trying to go. An interesting analogy from the age of technology! Elevators were one of the many wonders of Paris for this provincial girl from Lisieux. She was fourteen when her father took her and Céline to Paris and she discovered the joy of the elevator. On an interesting note, Bishop Ahern writes:

> Someone has consulted the roster of the hotel where the Martins stayed in Paris and discovered that Friedrich Nietzsche was a guest while they were there. One likes to imagine Nietzsche got into the elevator one day when Thérèse was trying it out. Bon jour, Monsieur, she would have said with her delightful smile to the father of modern atheism.[15] There is, of course, no way of verifying the possibility of a Thérèse—Nietzsche encounter.

Second, her "Little Way" of spiritual childhood. Thérèse's contribution has been described as a Copernican revolution in spirituality. "While she was an incomparably great mystic, a child can understand her. There are no flights of lofty rhetoric and no exaggerations in her writing. She had neither visions nor ecstasies."[16] Her little way was so very ordinary and undistinguished. She did not even have a Bible of her own in the

Carmel. Her knowledge of scripture would have come primarily from the Divine Office and the Mass. Her sister Céline copied most of the New Testament for her, as well as some Old Testament texts. A study of her biblical references shows that of the seventy-two books of the Bible, Thérèse made reference to fifty-two. That is extraordinary. She wished for the chance to study Greek and Hebrew so that she might read the sacred books in the languages in which they had been written and thus understand them better. Among her favorite Old Testament texts was Proverbs 9:4, which she read as "Whoever is a *little* one, let him come to me." Another was Isaiah 66:10–12, "As one whom a mother caresses, so will I comfort you; you shall be carried at the breasts, and upon the knees they will caress you."[17] This was the essence of her little way with God, the child in her littleness utterly trusting the divine Parent. Living today in an age of hermeneutic suspicion, it may be felt that this childlike simplicity and trust betrays no realistic appreciation of the psychological complexity of childhood. However, Aidan Nichols points out that in the total dependence of childhood complete trust of one's mother is necessary; he goes on to comment:

> Now this is interesting, because the archetypal child we once were (in that kind of way) is still alive in every one of us. To regress to it on the natural level would be a serious form of neurosis. To find our way back to it on the supernatural level is the highest form of maturity.[18]

Finding the way back to a basic and total trust in God as Father/Mother, and living out of that trust come what may, Thérèse's "Little Way," suggests not an infantile dependence but a mature recognition of the priority of grace, and of grace directed to the immediacy of one's person.

About six weeks before she died, Thérèse said to her sister Mother Agnes, "I feel my mission is to teach souls my little way." Mother Agnes asked, "What is this little way which you would teach souls?" "It is the way of spiritual childhood, the way of trust and absolute surrender." The way of total abandonment to the Father, in the Son, counting simply but absolutely on God to give us all that is necessary. No human being is ordinary for God, as it were. Each is loved by God uniquely and grows into an acceptance of the reality of the self as it is, as it is loved by God. Patrick Ahern comments:

> The Little Way finds joy in the present moment, in being pleased to be the person you are, whoever you are. It is a school of self-acceptance, which goes beyond *accepting* who you are to *wanting* to be who you are. It is a way of coming to terms with life both as it might be but as it is.[19]

Third, Thérèse's experience of the dark night. This little way of being the child of the Father, ever loved by him, remains central and constant in Thérèse's spiritual life. Noel Dermot O'Donoghue writes powerfully about this conviction: "Against all other notions of the deity Thérèse clung to this with unbreakable stubbornness. The only way that it might be put in question was through the very existence of God being put in question, and that is what happened at the end."[20] The experience of God's loving presence, the experience of God's very being departed. "[God]," Thérèse says, "permitted my soul to be invaded by the thickest darkness, and that the thought of heaven, up until then so sweet to me, be no longer anything but the cause of struggle and torment." She went through a long period of seemingly insurmountable doubts, lasting almost to the time of her death. "The veil of faith is almost torn aside; and yet it is no longer a veil for me, it is a wall which reaches right up to the heavens and covers the starry firmament." It was Thérèse's night of nothingness, her encounter with nihilism. She hears the darkness speaking to her: "You believe that one day you will walk out of this fog that surrounds you! Advance, advance; rejoice in death which will give you not what you hope for but a night still more profound, the night of nothingness."[21] Some thirty years before Heidegger or Sartre, Thérèse was using a phrase typical of them, "the night of nothingness."[22] Thérèse identified with the atheists as a result of this nihilistic, experience of utter darkness.

Maude Petre

Maude Dominica Petre (1863–1942), a modernist theological writer, spans both the nineteenth century and the twentieth, but, because of her connection with modernism, the treatment of her in the nineteenth century is amply justified—and the fact, already noted, that she was ten years older than St. Thérèse. Maude Petre came from a titled family, but both her parents died within months of each other when she was nineteen. Her family belonged to what has been called the *Cisalpine* wing of the church, that is to say, to those who were in favor of local control, of a measure of independence, much like the Gallican tradition of France. Cisalpine and Gallican stand against ultramontane.[23]

Maude's private tutors could hardly keep up with her developing intellect—in Nicholas Sagovsky's description she had "a kind of intellectual and moral fearlessness"[24]—and in 1885 she set off for Rome to study scholastic theology. Her aunt, Lady Lindsay, said of her at the time, "Maude has gone to Rome to study for the priesthood!"[25] In 1890 she entered the Society of the Daughters of the Heart of Mary in London. This was what would be known today as a lay institute. Petre remained with them until 1907, when she was dismissed for publishing a book entitled *Catholicism and Independence*—without permission.

Petre was the friend of a number of modernists, but especially of George Tyrrell. Though she had met Tyrrell several times before, it was on a retreat conducted by him in July 1900 that she came to be affected by him and to love him. She later wrote in her autobiography:

It was between thirty and forty…that I knew, in the complete sense, what it was to love…I had that consciousness of eternity; that sense that nothing else mattered on earth or in heaven; that it was the one priceless pearl for which all else could be sold or cast away as dross…that I could accept slavery or ill-treatment; that, finally, as I said to the one friend who guided me through this experience, I would "go to hell with him" if that was where he went.[26]

Tyrrell knew of her affection, but there is some evidence that he may have been homosexual.[27] Petre always attempted to purify her love, so that it would never be untoward. When all is said and done, however, in relation to Petre, Tyrrell veered between affection coupled with intellectual companionship and annoyance linked to frustration with her stifling devotion to him and her jealousy of any female competition.

Soon after this July retreat, Tyrrell went to live with the Jesuits in Richmond, Yorkshire, and he remained there until he left the Society in 1906. Petre, suffering from fatigue and depression as a result of her growing responsibilities in the Society of the Daughters of Mary, went for a rest to Engelberg, Switzerland, "where she went for long walks alone in the mountains and attended the Divine Office daily in the great Benedictine Abbey."[28] She made a perpetual vow of celibacy in 1901. When Tyrrell became seriously ill after he had been expelled from the Jesuits, she let him have a cottage on her property at Storrington, and it was there he died in 1909. She wrote over twelve books, mostly on Tyrrell, von Hügel, Loisy, and modernism generally.

During World War I, she served as a nurse in France and nursed the wounded from the bloody Battle of Verdun. She served as a fire warden at the time of the London blitz during World War II, even though she was almost eighty years old. She was an ardent spokesperson for social and spiritual issues and an advocate of the League of Nations. After her death in

London in 1942, there was a requiem Mass in Assumption Convent, Kensington Square, the Archdiocese of Westminster. She was buried not far from George Tyrrell in the Anglican cemetery of Storrington. Bishop Peter Amigo of the Diocese of Southwark did not permit a priest to attend the graveside services because Maude Petre was being laid to rest but one grave removed from her friend Fr. George Tyrrell.[29]

The Theology of Maude Petre

Maude Petre's theology is complex and in so many ways caught up in the turmoil of modernism. Nonetheless, it is possible to give some sense of her thinking without descending to great detail. In an early essay published in the Jesuit periodical *The Month,* she sets out a theme that will permeate much of her later work: ordinary human thought and experience are the primary places for locating the things of God.[30] This was in contrast to a supernatural extrinsicism that views the transcendent reality of God alongside human experience. For Petre God is immanent, and yet not to the point where God's transcendence is compromised into a form of pantheism.[31] The encyclical *Pascendi* would condemn "vital immanence," but Petre's theology would not fall under that condemnation. She understood the reality of divine transcendence well enough.

Ecclesiology was a concern of hers, especially from the years 1901–1902, focusing on the relationship of the church to the modern world. One contemporary commentator sees in Petre something of an anticipation of Vatican II: "Her ecclesiology roamed freely over questions of asceticism, discipline, mission, and reform. Such writings anticipated the call of the Second Vatican Council for a church *semper reformanda*— always in need of reform."[32] In a letter of 1923 to Lord Halifax, the peer who enthusiastically promoted Anglican union with Rome, Petre wrote of the church: "The Church is our home— our ark on the immeasured waters. We know that we know but little, but we trust that the spiritual goods set before us are a pledge of those that are to be."[33] No one would take issue with her ecclesiology thus far.

However, when she was seen to be calling into question the authority of the church, that was another matter. In December 1907 both her religious superior and the archbishop of Westminster, Francis Bourne, asked Petre to withdraw from publication her book *Catholicism and Independence*. She maintained that this was impossible, and as a result, her connection with the institute was terminated. The reason may be clearly seen in the opening pages of the book: "To our own mental and moral conscience all doctrines and laws must make their last appeal."[34] Petre's approach to doctrine and morality can hardly be construed as anarchist. Rather, we may see in this statement a reflection of her Cisalpine heritage, her own independence of mind, as well as the general, though limited, influence of modernist thinking. Give the temper of the times, this was enough to draw deeper the suspicion under which she already labored as a result of her association and friendship with George Tyrrell. *Catholicism and Independence* sounded like the entire liberal agenda of the nineteenth century in modernist dress. Petre appreciated and respected the church's role in faith and morals, but it was for her a qualified role: "The Church has lighted my way. Instead of struggle through a wilderness I have had a road—a road to virtue and truth. Only a road—the road to an end, not the end itself—the road to truth, and not the fullness of truth itself."[35] Her distance from a superficial doctrinal relativism may be found in this statement: "To be undenominational and consequently tolerant is nothing; but to be denominational in the best sense, and likewise tolerant, is much."[36] No espousal here of a lazy, anti-intellectual tolerance, but rather tolerance as the recognition of intellectually convinced denominationalism that can from a position of strength engage with other points of view. These were not things the Catholic hierarchy of England wanted to hear at this time of the condemnation of modernism.

Although her own bishop, Peter Amigo of Southwark, refused her holy communion in any parish of the diocese, all Petre had to do was cross the River Thames and she was in the Archdiocese of Westminster, and there she could receive the Eucharist without difficulty or impediment. She did so almost on a daily basis.

Conclusion

Thérèse Martin was made a saint in 1925, and a doctor of the church in 1997, the centenary of her death, by Pope John Paul II. She is, as Aidan Nichols has it, "A teacher of faith and morals—Christian believing and Christian living—worthy to be mentioned in the same breath as an Augustine or a Basil."[37] There is a huge Theresian industry of research and publication. While there continues to be some interest in the modest contribution of Maude Petre, it pales in insignificance alongside Thérèse. That is entirely proper, given the ecclesial recognition of Thérèse's sanctity and doctoral status. At the same time, the church must continue to exemplify the intellectual inquisitiveness, the moral fiber and courage of such as Maude Petre. In von Hügel's terms, the mystical may be finally the most important of the dimensions of religion, but even recognizing that to be the case is dependent on the intellectual dimension. Both Thérèse and Maude have their rightful place among our "great cloud of witnesses" (Heb 12:1).

Bibliography

Crews, Clyde F. *English Catholic Modernism: Maude Petre's Way of Faith*. Notre Dame, IN: University of Notre Dame Press, 1984.

Thérèse of Lisieux. *Story of a Soul: The Autobiography of Thérèse of Lisieux*. 3rd ed. Washington, DC: ICS Publications, 1996.

Notes

1. Aidan Nichols, OP, *A Spirituality for the Twenty-first Century* (Huntington, IN: Our Sunday Visitor Publishing Division, 2003), 17.

2. Maude Petre, *My Way of Faith* (London: J. M. Dent and Sons, 1937), 235.

3. Nichols, *Spirituality for the Twenty-first Century,* 19.

4. Hans Urs von Balthasar, *Thérèse of Lisieux: The Story of a Mission* (New York/London: Sheed and Ward, 1953), 157–59.

5. Ida Goerres, *The Hidden Face: A Study of St. Thérèse of Lisieux* (London: Burns and Oates, 1959), 260–61.

6. See David F. Ford, *Self and Salvation: Being Transformed* (Cambridge: Cambridge University Press, 1999), 229.

7. Goerres, *Hidden Face,* 13.

8. Patrick Ahern, *Maurice and Thérèse: The Story of a Love* (New York/London: Doubleday, 1998), 15.

9. Thérèse of Lisieux, *Story of a Soul: The Autobiography of St. Thérèse of Lisieux,* 3rd ed. (Washington, DC: ICS Publications, 1996), 194. See also Louis Bouyer, CO, *Women Mystics* (San Francisco: Ignatius Books, 1993), 149–50; and Ford, *Self and Salvation,* 230.

10. Cited in Ahern, *Maurice and Thérèse,* 113.

11. Ahern, *Maurice and Thérèse,* 114.

12. Ibid., 140.

13. Noel Dermot O'Donoghue, ODC, *Mystics for Our Time* (Wilmington, DE: Michael Glazier, 1989), 116.

14. Ahern, *Maurice and Thérèse,* 166.

15. Ibid., 174.

16. Ibid., 147.

17. Thérèse, *Story of a Soul,* 188.

18. Nichols, *Spirituality for the Twenty-first Century,* 26.

19. Ahern, *Maurice and Thérèse,* 114.

20. Noel Demot O'Donoghue, *Heaven in Ordinarie* (Edinburgh: T. & T. Clark, 1979), 73.

21. Thérèse, *Story of a Soul,* 211, 214, 213.

22. O'Donoghue, *Mystics for Our Time,* 122.

23. Maude could have found, maintains Francis Oakley, relief in conciliarism during her own period of anguish and difficulties with ecclesiastical authority. That she did not shows how marginalized conciliarist constitutionalism had become in Catholic ecclesiology and church history in the wake of Vatican I. See Francis Oakley, *The Conciliarist Tradition* (New York/Oxford: Oxford University Press, 2003), 251.

24. Nicholas Sagovsky, *'On God's Side': A Life of George Tyrrell* (Oxford: Clarendon Press, 1990), 57.

25. Maude Petre, *Modernism: Its Failure and Its Fruits* (London: T. C. and E. C. Jack, 1918), 56.

26. Petre, *My Way of Faith,* 129–30.

27. In 1897 he began a correspondence with Andre Raffalovich in which he felt free to reveal that his most passionate feelings as a younger man had been directed to members of the same sex. See Meriol Trevor, *Prophets and Guardians: Renewal and Tradition in the Church* (London/Sydney/Toronto: Hollis and Carter, 1969), 35–36; and Sagovsky, *'On God's Side',* 67.

28. Trevor, *Prophets and Guardians,* 30.

29. Clyde F. Crews, *English Catholic Modernism: Maude Petre's Way of Faith* (Notre Dame, IN: University of Notre Dame Press, 1984), 99. Crews's book is an excellent guide to Petre's thought.

30. Maude Petre, "An Englishwoman's Love Letters," *The Month* (February 1901): 120–24.

31. See Crews, *English Catholic Modernism,* 17.

32. Ibid., 21.

33. Cited in Crews, *English Catholic Modernism,* 104.

34. Maude Petre, *Catholicism and Independence* (London: Longmans Green, 1907), x–xi.

35. Thérèse, *My Way of Faith,* 341.

36. Petre, *Catholicism and Independence,* 158.

37. Nichols, *Spirituality for the Twenty-first Century,* 17.

CONCLUSION

The church is best understood as communion, the sacrament of communion with the Triune God, and the sacrament of communion among people.[1] This side of heaven the ecclesial communion is made up of imperfect people, failing, weeping, but creeping toward the throne of grace. This imperfect species is made up of conservatives, progressives or liberals, and of all shades of in-between, but all of them strive to love God within the communion of the church. Their communion is real; they are united but not uniform. Nor do they need to be uniform. The communion of the church is broad enough, catholic enough, to include all, and our soundings in the nineteenth-century church have confirmed this.

This book began with the historian Meriol Trevor, and in the conclusion we return to her. Trevor wrote: "Now that we have glanced at a few people in past critical situations, perhaps our own crisis may appear less sudden, less obscure. Since the eighteenth century the same questions, in varying forms, have faced the Church...."[2] The tensions in the church of today are the tensions of yesterday and the tensions of every day. The church is made up of guardians, prophets, and saints. The guardians are the conservatives; the prophets are the progressives; and the saints speak for themselves. Or do they? From the historical soundings we have taken there is one *Blessed,* Pius IX, and two *Saints,* Thérèse of Lisieux and Pius X, and the canonization process moves ahead slowly for John Henry Newman.

It is revealing to note that the pope who summoned the Second Vatican Council, Blessed John XXIII, had himself been suspected of modernism through using the historical work of Monsignor Louis Duchesne, as has been noted earlier. When he became pope, Angelo Roncalli found a file about himself in the records of the Holy Office (now the Congregation for the Doctrine of the Faith) with the words "Suspected of Modernism" written against his name. As Pope John XXIII, Roncalli took a pen and wrote in the record, "I was never a Modernist."[3]

Trevor continues:

> The movements which at last flowered into full acceptance at the Second Vatican Council, social, liturgical, historical, ecumenical, theological, were all started during that period, and in spite of the setbacks that followed *Pascendi,* they all survived. The next generations learnt from the pioneers who had the patience to stay in the Church, in spite of the treatment meted out to them by the suspicious authorities.[4]

The reference to Pope Pius X's encyclical letter *Pascendi* shows clearly that Trevor is speaking specifically of modernism. But may we not take her excellent point and extend it, with appropriate qualification, to the entire nineteenth century?

Möhler's communion ecclesiology finds full acceptance in the documents of Vatican II and in the development of post-conciliar versions of communion ecclesiology.[5] Papal infallibility as proclaimed by Vatican I during the pontificate of Pope Pius IX finds not only its complement but its flourishing in the doctrine of episcopal collegiality of Vatican II, and in the development of episcopal conferences since then. Many of John Henry Newman's ideas permeate the pages of *Lumen Gentium,* not least his acceptance of the central role of the laity in the church. His concern for preaching and Hopkins's love for word crafting find an echo in Vatican II's insistence on the importance of preaching in the life of a priest or a bishop. Isaac Hecker's optimistic vision of the church surely finds expression in the vibrant, if sometimes polarized, American church of today. The social teaching of Pope Leo XIII finds continuity and development in Pope John Paul II's *Centesimus Annus*. Without accepting egregiously erroneous aspects of modernists, the church has adapted to some of their genuine insights in the wake of the conciliar renewal, for example, in the study of scripture, in recognizing the historical development of doctrine. The church has continued to deepen and advance the liturgical renewal found in Pope Pius X, while distancing itself from the way he handled modernism. Thérèse of Lisieux's spirituality, the little way of love, continues to attract millions, and not only Roman Catholics. The Maude Petres of our times are students of theology all over the world and are making a substantial contribution to the renewal of the church. Finally, von Hügel shows us perhaps a way to live with the tensions between the institutional, intellectual, and mystical dimensions of what it means to be a Catholic in the twenty-first century.

In other words, a real sense of church history liberates and challenges us, and we ignore it at our peril. The last word should go to Meriol Trevor: "Above all, from history we can discover again the necessity of remaining in communion: no one can be a Christian alone, and we owe everything to this holy and living tradition of the Church."[6]

Notes

1. *Lumen Gentium* 1.

2. Meriol Trevor, *Prophets and Guardians, Renewal and Tradition in the Church* (London/Sydney/Toronto: Hollis and Carter, 1969), 201.

3. Ibid., 205.

4. Ibid., 90.

5. Dennis Doyle offers various models of communion ecclesiology, and is particularly good on Möhler (*Communion Ecclesiology: Visions and Versions* [Maryknoll, NY: Orbis Books, 2000]).

6. Trevor, *Prophets and Guardians*, 209.